TWAYNE'S WORLD AUTHORS SERIES

A Survey of the World's Literature

Sylvia E. Bowman, Indiana University

GENERAL EDITOR

SPAIN

Gerald E. Wade, Vanderbilt University
Janet Winecoff Díaz, University of North Carolina at Chapel Hill

EDITORS

Enrique Jardiel Poncela

TWAS 333

Enrique Jardiel Poncela

Enrique Jardiel Poncela

By DOUGLAS R. McKAY

*University of Colorado,
Colorado Springs*

Twayne Publishers, Inc.   ::   New York

Library of Congress Cataloging in Publication Data

McKay, Douglas R
    Enrique Jardiel Poncela.

    (Twayne's world authors series, TWAS 333. Spain)
    Bibliography: p. 111.
    1. Jardiel Poncela, Enrique, 1901–1952.
PQ6619.A7Z8   862'.6'2   74-6487
ISBN 0–8057–2462–1

To Mac and Alice

Contents

About the Author

Douglas R. McKay is Associate Professor of Spanish and Chairman of the Department of Foreign Language and Literature at the University of Colorado, Colorado Springs. He received his B.A. degree in 1962 from the University of Utah, his M.A. in 1964 from the University of Oregon, and his Ph.D. in 1968 from Michigan State University. He has resided in Uruguay for thirty months, in Spain for one year, and again in Spain, Mexico, and France over several summers.

Professor McKay is the author of a Twayne critical biography on Carlos Arniches (1972) and editor of *Misterio y pavor: Trece cuentos* (Holt, Rinehart and Winston, 1974). His book reviews and articles have appeared in *Books Abroad, Choice, The Explicator, Hispania, Latin America Literary Review, The Modern Language Journal,* and *Modern Language Notes.* He is currently serving as Review Editor for Spanish publications on the staff of *The Modern Language Journal.*

Preface

Enrique Jardiel Poncela (1901–1952) had intended to revolutionize the literary world with his unconventional approach to humor. He died convinced that he would have achieved that ideal had it not been for the excoriation of his uncompromising enemies of the press. While indeed he was severely berated throughout the last twenty years of his life, most of the professional adversity he encountered was avoidable; it grew in direct proportion to his own emotional overreaction to criticism. Allowing his detractors' negative judgment to undermine his artistic resolve, Jardiel misspent many precious years of creative talent in a relentless endeavor to justify himself before his public. Thus, some of the sweeping changes he had determined to make miscarried because of his personal struggle for vindication.

Today, however, a large segment of the Spanish critical press has shifted its sentiment from displeasure to reverence. Many leading playwrights declare their indebtedness to Jardiel's example and talent and, above all, to those unique revolutionary intentions that so exasperated the Spanish theater world for a score of years before and after the Spanish Civil War. Those who witnessed the ruthless attacks on his plays and novels one generation ago would marvel to see the long swing of the pendulum move slowly away from disapproval and scorn towards veneration. The few writers, critics, and playgoers who then constituted the "Jardielesque" camp, an assemblage fraught with controversy, uncertain of its impact on literature and troubled by the crass mediocrity of so much easy laughter and facile comic situations, would now look hopefully to the day when Jardiel may be remembered as the unrivaled master of the absurd and the bizarre in Spanish theater humor.

The present study tries to meet the pro-*jardielistas* halfway in their defense of *jardielismo*. We are aware of the man's innovative flair, his unassailable energy, his remarkable creative talent, and the fact that his labors once held the promise that he would become one of the stellar figures of the contemporary drama of the absurd. But we also recognize the man's limitations as a playwright and novelist. As we attempt to evaluate the literary impact of his accomplishments, we are constantly reminded that Jardiel fell far short of his intended goals, having strained too hard on the side of extravagance and excess. And in this realization there persists that unfixed ambivalence of a value judgment which tends, on the one hand, to acclaim Jardiel for his valiant effort, and on the other hand, to reproach him for his collapse in the midst of preventable tribulations that he himself had labored to provoke.

Several individuals have been gracious and generous with their time in contributing to the substance of this study. My appreciation is due particularly to Evangelina Jardiel Poncela for her encouragement and a provision of valuable data. To Alfredo Marquerie I extend a warm and special expression of gratitude. And to my dear skeptical friend, Miguel Mihura, my thanks again for granting me the warmth of his kind hospitality and allowing me to understand Jardiel from a different point of view. A cooperative response to my constant needling for information about Jardiel Poncela's present-day influence came, both by mail and by way of personal contact, from the following individuals, to whom also I express appreciation: Arcadio Baquero Goyanes, Antonio Buero Vallejo, Joaquín Calvo Sotelo, Juan Emilio Aragonés, José López Rubio, Lauro Olmo, Alfonso Paso, José María Pemán, Adolfo Prego, Víctor Ruíz Iriarte, and Alfonso Sastre. My thanks go as well to members of the Sección de Difusión de la Dirección General de Cultura Popular y Espectáculos, Ministerio de Información y Turismo, Madrid, especially Miguel Ortega, Cesáreo Andrés Alonso, and Rafael Hierro Rojo; and to Carlos Salleras, General Secretary of the Asociación Española de la Prensa Técnica y Periódica; and finally, to the hard-working personnel of Madrid's Hemeroteca Nacional.

Materially, the preparation for this study was aided by a grant-in-aid from the University of Colorado's Council on Research and Creative work, for whose generosity I once again express appreciation.

DOUGLAS R. McKAY

University of Colorado, Colorado Springs

Chronology

1901 October 15: Jardiel Poncela born in Madrid.
1916 Begins a ten-year playwriting collaboration with Serafín Adame Martínez.
1917 Death of Marcelina Poncela, Jardiel's mother.
1919 Jardiel and Adame Martínez stage their first play.
1926 Begins career as independent playwright following rupture with Adame Martínez.
1927 May 28: Première of *A Sleepless Spring Night* (*Una noche de primavera sin sueño*). First published book: *Pirulís of Havana* (*Pirulís de la Habana*), a collection of his short stories. First film: Adaptation of Arniches' *Es mi hombre*.
1929 Publishes his first major novel, *Love Is Written Without The Letter 'H'* (*Amor se escribe sin hache*).
1930 Publication of second novel, *Wait for Me in Siberia, My Love!* (*¡Espérame en Siberia, vida mía!*).
1931 Publication of third novel, *Eleven Thousand Virgins* (*Pero..., ¿hubo alguna vez once mil vírgenes?*).
1932 Jardiel publishes his fourth and final novel, *The Tour of God* (*La 'tournée' de Dios*). September: Begins his first residence in Hollywood, under contract with Fox Film Corporation.
1933 First volume of plays: *Three Comedies with One Essay* (*Tres comedias con un solo ensayo*).
1934 March 2: Première of *Angelina, or A Brigadier's Honor* (*Angelina, o El honor de un brigadier*). July: Begins second residence in Hollywood.
1935 Publishes his second volume of plays:: *Angelina*.
1936 May 2: Première of *Four Hearts in Check and Backward March* (*Cuatro corazones con freno y marcha atrás*). Third volume of plays: *Forty-nine Characters Who Found Their Author* (*Cuarenta y nueve personajes que encontraron a su autor*).

1937 August 24: Departs for Buenos Aires during Spanish Civil War.

1938 Publishes *The Convalescent's Book* (*El libro del convaleciente*) a miscellany of quips, anecdotes, and stories.

1939 Fourth volume of plays: *Two Farces and One Operetta* (*Dos farsas y una opereta*). October 21: Première of *A Round-Trip Husband* (*Un marido de ida y vuelta*).

1940 May 24: Première of Jardiel's most celebrated play, *Heloise Lies under an Almond Tree* (*Eloísa está debajo de un almendro*). First theater tour through northern Spain as director of his own company.

1941 April 15: Première of *We Thieves Are Honorable People* (*Los ladrones somos gente honrada*).

1942 Fifth volume of plays: *One Protested Draft and Two at Sight* (*Una letra protestada y dos letras a la vista*). Second theater tour within Spain as director of his own company.

1943 February 16: Première of *Blanca on the Outside and Rosa Within* (*Blanca por fuera y Rosa por dentro*). Publishes *Excess Baggage* (*Exceso de equipaje*), a collection of stories, lectures, and reminiscences.

1944 Sixth volume of plays: *Three Projectiles from '42* (*Tres proyectiles del 42*). Theater tour with his own company to Buenos Aires.

1945 March 16: Première of *You and I Make Three* (*Tú y yo somos tres*).

1946 Seventh volume of plays: *From Blanca to the Cat by Way of the Boulevard* (*De Blanca al gato, pasando por el bulevár*). Eighth and final volume of plays: *Water, Oil and Gasoline and Two Other Explosive Mixtures* (*Agua, aceite y gasolina y otras dos mezclas explosivas*). Receives the coveted Jacinto Benavente Award for *The Weaker Sex Has Undergone Gymnastics* (*El sexo débil ha hecho gimnasia*), voted the best play of 1946.

1952 February 18: Jardiel dies in Madrid following a prolonged illness.

CHAPTER 1

Life and Times of
Enrique Jardiel Poncela

THE literary career of Enrique Jardiel Poncela was so agitated, so fraught with misunderstandings and turmoil, that honest biographical reporting has been profoundly affected. Only Jardiel's immediate family, close friends, and supporters have attempted to record the events of his life, but their efforts have resulted, at best, in impassioned vindications of the playwright's defensive posture before his enemies. Juan Bonet's tiresome harangue[1] reads like a courtroom appeal for acquittal, while Rafael Flórez's two pretentious monographs[2] are replete with heavy platitudes, empty adulation, and fallacious data. Evangelina Jardiel Poncela, seeking to reproach Flórez for his many inexcusable blunders, has published the most recent document on her father's life,[3] but even her emotionally-charged apology, sensitive and personal to the extreme, leaves many questions unanswered and tends only to clarify minor inaccuracies in its resolve to justify the playwright's neurotic tendencies.

The earnest biographer might turn, in desperation and with some willing suspension of disbelief, to Jardiel's own writings, hopeful of gleaning useful facts hidden among the writer's bombastic declamations and the amusing reminiscences that pervade his celebrated prologues to the published plays. Yet here again the issuance of detailed data is tinged with suspect exaggeration, calculated to amuse rather than inform the reader. Jardiel had long intended to write his autobiography, a book that would have been titled *Symphony in Me* (*Sinfonía en mí*), but the project, like the forty unfinished plays he left in his folio at the time of his death, never materialized beyond an outline form. He did write several "Self-portraits" ("Autorretratos"), most in verse form, and he even conducted a series of "Self-interviews"

13

("Auto-entrevistas"), incorporated in his published prologues. These provide valuable insights into Jardiel's literary purpose, but generally they repeat the same sketchy line of autobiographical information found in the prologues.

The basic name-and-date facts about Jardiel's life are readily available, of course, but the tempestuous spirit of the man himself has never been fully revealed. The real frustrations that prompted his public rage against certain individuals and engendered his later paranoia, the man's secret liaisons and multiple amorous adventures, his obsession with the fear of an early death with a corresponding emotional tie to his mother's graveside, his uncommon broodings, the unparalleled rejoicings—these constitute a part of the many undivulged components of his life which emerge only as shadows to taunt the reader. It is perhaps true, as several critics have averred, that Jardiel spoke and wrote more about himself than has any other literary figure in the history of Spain, but it must be added that he said very little about the real Jardiel. His autobiographical musings afford nothing beyond a humorous soliloquy concerning his exterior impudence and surface capers. They provide many facts about his problems with play production and the creative process. They supply us as well with the names of his friends and enemies, the titles of the cafés where he wrote, and the creeds which governed the exercise of his artistic life. But Jardiel Poncela, the troubled, tormented, unhappy man who died in great pain, profound despair, and utter loneliness, remains marvelously concealed. Every person who suffers and loves deeply should enjoy the right to live and to die with his life unexposed. This privilege still belongs to Jardiel Poncela.

I *Jardiel's Youth*

Jardiel was born on October 15, 1901, at 31-33 Arco de Santa María, now Augusto Figueroa Street, Madrid. He was the fourth child and only son of Marcelina Poncela and Enrique Jardiel.[4] His father, a quiet, reserved, undistinguished man, was employed as a court reporter and in time became editor of *La Correspondencia de España*, a now defunct newspaper. Jardiel frequently accompanied him to the "Cortes," or the Spanish

Parliament, and then to the newspaper office, and thus he acquired his enthusiasm for journalism at an early age. His mother, a sensitive, cultured woman who encouraged her son to read widely and to visit art museums, was herself an accomplished painter who conducted art classes in the home. Jardiel was especially close to Doña Marcelina. When she died of cancer in the summer of 1917, the effect on her teenage boy was profound and damaging. Her memory was constantly present in his thoughts and, for many years, whenever Jardiel was deeply troubled, he sought comfort and strength by visiting her grave in Quinto del Ebro.

In the prologue to his first published novel,[5] Jardiel discusses his disorderly, undisciplined upbringing. He tells us that his readings were intense but sporadic. They included such authors as Aristophanes, Dante, Conan Doyle, Dumas, Kant, Ovid, and Jules Verne. His education reflected the same random exposure to various schools and varied philosophies of instruction, a mixture he characterized as "explosive." From the age of four to seven he attended the influential Free Institution of Teaching, directed by the famous pedagogue, Don Francisco Giner de los Ríos. He then spent four years at Madrid's French *Lycée*. This was followed, from the age of eleven through sixteen, by rigorous academic study at the Institute of the Fathers Escolapios of San Antonio Abad. The final year of his high school training took place at the Institute of Cardenal Cisneros.

Jardiel was a mischievous student. His varied reading and good memory enabled him to obtain good grades, but his restless spirit troubled his mentors and involved him in a series of minor student fracases. This penchant for tumult at the expense of serious study accompanied Jardiel through two wasted years at the University of Madrid's Facultad de Filosofía y Letras. He finally abandoned higher education for a salaried job in his father's newspaper office and as a reporter on the staff of *La Acción*.

Jardiel's attention had turned resolutely to theater writing—all for fun and nothing for profit—when he was midway through his *bachillerato* training. At the age of fifteen his family moved to an apartment on Churruca Street, where Jardiel befriended Serafín Adame Martínez, a fat, precocious neighbor who shared his enthusiasm for play productions. In the ten years to follow, Jardiel and his pudgy collaborator wrote over thirty full-length plays together. This youthful theater apprenticeship with Adame Martínez was in fact the culmination of many childhood hours in which Jardiel had played theater games with his sisters; as a very young boy, his favorite pastime had been the collection of small props and the staging of simple plays. Indeed, Jardiel had so succumbed to the self-imposed literary fever which pervaded his boyhood leisure time while on vacation from school, that at the age of eleven he had written the first of several historical romantic novels, a book he entitled *Montsalud de Brievas*. This was followed by a large number of plays and several folios of poetry.[6]

For several years following his departure from formal education, Jardiel worked by day as a news correspondent and wrote plays at night with Adame Martínez. Even though he later repudiated his hodgepodge of stories, novels, plays, articles, and poems of this period as "odious, putrid, and repugnant,"[7] he and his neighbor friend eventually produced a play worthy of production. In 1919, a director named Enrique Rambal consented to stage their four-act farce, *Prince Raudhick* (*El príncipe Raudhick*), at Bilbao's Trueba Theater. The play was mildly successful, enough to encourage the two promising playwrights to stage it again, this time in the nation's capital. It was scheduled for a short run at Madrid's aging Gran Teatro on Marqués de la Ensenada Street, but shortly before opening night, the old theater burned to the ground. Undaunted, the teenage authors returned to their attic studio to continue writing. Jardiel thus spent the late years of his adolescence laboring long into the night on dozens of frivolous adventure plays, anticipating the moment when he would be able to formulate his own unique and independent style.

II *His Career*

1926 was a decisive year for Jardiel. His prolonged initiation into theater writing with Adame Martínez came to an abrupt end and he faced the inevitability of striking out on his own. Still in high gear after many years of constant productivity, he set to work writing his first comedy as an independent playwright. The work, *A Sleepless Spring Night* (*Una noche de primavera sin sueño*) was staged in May of 1927, with a success that imbued Jardiel with dreams to revolutionize the entire course of theater humor in Spain. His ambition to enrich drama with a new, revivifying line of talent also splashed over into the field of prose fiction. Soon after Jardiel met José Ruiz-Castillo, the editor of Madrid's Biblioteca Nueva, which featured the publication of humorous novels, he devoted ten months to the preparation of two comic narratives, *Love Is Written Without the Letter 'H'* (*Amor se escribe sin hache*) and *Wait for Me in Siberia, My Love* (*Espérame en Siberia, vida mía*). During the ensuing four years, Jardiel balanced his production equally between the staging of several full-length plays and the issuance of two additional novels, *Eleven Thousand Virgins* (*Pero...¿hubo alguna vez once mil vírgenes?*) and *The Tour of God* (*La "tournée" de Dios*).

Jardiel's novelistic ventures assured him an important place among a generation of humorists headed by Ramón Gómez de la Serna and Wenceslao Fernández Flórez.[8] He shared their enthusiasm for carrying comic expression to the maximum limits of exaggeration, deformation, and caricature. But while his own contributions to the genre were successful in a commercial sense, he fell far short of being an extraordinary novelist, and soon grew weary of the challenge. Still determined, however, to reform the literary scene, he adopted comedy as his métier and looked to both the stage and the cinema as his principal modes of artistic expression.

Some years earlier, Jardiel had begun a series of literary contributions to a newly-founded weekly periodical named *Buen Humor*. These writings, prepared in close association with the future playwright, José López Rubio, afforded Jardiel an opportunity to assess the public's reaction to his humoristic posture. More important, as his friendship with López Rubio solidified, the two men abandoned the journal to collaborate in writing two three-act comedies.[9] From this venture, López Rubio gravitated to cinematographic work, accepting a contract in August of 1930 to write Spanish dialogue for MGM Studios in Hollywood. Jardiel followed López Rubio's cinematic example, but spread his own creative impulses over a wider range of activity in Madrid, flitting from screen adaptations to script writings, from the publication of short stories and humorous articles to a series of popular radio conferences, from playwriting to public lectures.[10] When he culminated these many labors with an original screen play, A Prisoner Has Escaped (Se ha fugado un preso), López Rubio, who was still residing in Hollywood, helped secure for his friend a film-making contract with Fox Film Corporation. Thus, Jardiel Poncela sailed for his first of two visits to the United States in September of 1932.

Jardiel spent a total of nearly twenty months in Hollywood. His special tasks were to assist in the production of Spanish films, composing Spanish dialogue for American films, offering technical advice, and supervising the filming of one of his own sucessful plays, Angelina, or A Brigadier's Honor (Angelina, o El honor de un brigadier). The bizarre aspects of life in Hollywood made a lasting impression on Jardiel; he responded to the stimuli of unusual occurrences and strange habits, of exciting capitalist mores and shocking life styles, by publishing a series of short essays called My Travels in the United States (Mis viajes a los Estados Unidos)[11] and by producing the colossal failure of his dramatic repertory, Love Lasts Only 2000 Meters (El amor sólo dura 2000 metros).

The Hollywood experience was highlighted by a "discovery" that Jardiel long considered to be his most significant contribution to cinematographic innovations. Reportedly, Jardiel was the first person to take an old silent film and add a sound track of humorous commentary to the action.[12] He went back almost thirty years in time to dig out film classics of the silent picture era. With clever editing and the addition of sound, Jardiel repopularized these short films under the amusing title, Rancid Celluloid (Celuloide rancio).[13] This achievement brought Jardiel fame as a pioneer of cinematic art in Spain, along with López Rubio and Edgar Neville.

Jardiel was slow to forsake his film work, even upon his final departure from Hollywood in April of 1935. The outbreak of the Spanish Civil War interrupted several cinematic contracts in Barcelona, as it brought to a momentary close much of his journalistic work. In fact, he had already determined to turn almost exclusively to stage comedy, since it represented, he said, the supreme manifestation of his intelligence. Indeed, his playwriting activities were so intense as the Civil War commenced, in the summer of 1936, that he had already initiated a private battle all his own with many Madrilenean critics, most of whom greeted his egotistical pronouncements and unusual productions with adverse press notices.

Although Jardiel's sentiments during the Spanish Civil War were definitely pro-Franco,[14] he chose to live for several months, midway through the conflagration, in Buenos Aires. His Argentine residence was characterized by the same tireless energy that preceded and followed the period of temporary self-exile. He supervised the filming of his play *Margarita, Armando and His Father* (*Margarita, Armando y su padre*), delivered a series of nine lectures on Radio Rivadavia, and arranged the production of two new plays. Upon returning to Spain in 1940, he combined another brief involvement with film work, consisting of a second series of silent pictures, with commentary, entitled *Comic Celluloids* (*Celuloides cómicos*), undertaken in San Sebastián, with his first tour as director of his own theater company, which enjoyed a complete artistic and financial success touring the northern provinces of Spain.[15]

In the years to follow, Jardiel Poncela's career mushroomed under a constant flux and flow of major theater activity. He produced many plays, some with a success unparalleled in his time, others of such catastrophic disappointment that his critics never forgave him his failures during his entire lifetime. He also continued to adapt some of his comedies for motion pictures, delivered more lectures, wrote more articles, and eventually, in 1944, returned to Buenos Aires with his own theater company. On the surface, these events would suggest that Jardiel was at the pinnacle of enjoying immense financial rewards and professional esteem for his labors. His exuberant imagination and uninhibited creativity had earned him the respect of his colleagues in the theater world and the outspoken admiration of such prominent figures as Eugenio d'Ors, Alfredo Marqueríe, and Gómez de la Serna. But a tragic flaw in his character had also unleashed the harpies of the local press to taunt and torment him with their adverse comments. Jardiel, blind to his own excesses, intolerant of criticism, certain of the immortality of his artistic contributions, became, during the final decade of his life, a disconsolate victim to the acerbic attacks of his unseen critics and the vociferous heckling of the so-called *antijardielistas*, the angry spectators who demonstrated their resistance to everything he believed in with such intensity that their protests made difficult a fair hearing on the worth of the playwright's work. The bitterness of his overreaction to their forays affected Jardiel's mental, emotional, and physical health perceptibly. He died in Madrid, February 18, 1952.

III   *Jardiel and the Critics: Twenty Years of Contention*

The sneers and slurs of ceaseless dissent from his critics embittered the life of Enrique Jardiel Poncela. From the time of his first major stage success until the end of his days, Jardiel's name and labor were deprecated by an unforgiving press. The early indifference of some drama critics and spectators shifted in time to disparagement, while the insults of his most implacable foes had magnified by 1946 into a public outburst of belligerence and scorn probably unparalleled in the history of the Spanish theater.

The life and writings of Jardiel cannot accurately be appraised without reference to the polemics that raged for nearly twenty years between the playwright and his aggressive critics.[16] So brutal was the censure against him and so intrepid his own sarcasm to counter the derision, that Jardiel's last years were clouded by anguish, his spirit broken, his health impaired. Some of his writings were marred by the intensity of his displeasure and the attitude of extreme defensiveness he felt compelled to assume. With each new self-justifying retort, Jardiel grew more vulnerable to the punishing tirades of his detractors. All too often, in his enthusiasm to uphold his personal dramatic creed, he allowed the irreverance of his counterattack to fall on specific individuals, thus fomenting, in addition to the incessant battle over issues, a personal war with several influential personalities of Madrilenean theater life.

Jardiel's apologists have explained in several ways the causes of his disaffection with his critics. For some, the playwright's

anger was the result of recurring financial reversals. There may
be some truth to this viewpoint. Jardiel tended on occasion to
lash out in self-defense when pressures mounted. He often accused short-sighted critics for inciting his box-office failures with
their negative reviews. "First you wound my pride, then you
plunder my purse," was his occasional charge. Perhaps Jardiel
needed such enemies: they served his need for a scapegoat, a
transference mechanism to collective foes of the fourth estate
for his own feelings of ineptitude, insecurity, or inadequacy.

Others have cited Jardiel's increasing ill health over the last
two decades of his life as giving rise to a fierce emotional defiance in the face of the adverse criticism. This state of mind was
especially made manifest in the final months of his life, when
severe physical pain exacerbated his hostility to such an extent
that he absolutely refused to see or to speak with anyone outside
of his immediate family and one or two old friends.

Still other have viewed Jardiel as a victim of a kind of
Weltschmerz. He is sometimes referred to as a man chronically
saddened by life's struggles, the Spanish Civil War, political
tyranny, and unhappy love affairs.[17] Nonetheless, Jardiel was,
according to his closest friends and relatives, anything but a
hardened misanthrope or brooding melancholic. His daughters
attest to his cordial manners, kindly disposition, generosity, and
optimistic outlook. Whatever bitterness he may have manifested
was reserved, it seems, for his implacable enemies of the press.

The best explanation for Jardiel's undaunted warfare with
drama critics would appear to be that of his own restless refusal
to remain silent vis-à-vis any real or anticipated adverse criticism.
There was something deeply entrenched in his nature that cried
out for combat. The published prologues to his plays underline
the hostility he experienced, the antagonisms he invited, and the
enmity or allegiance he expressed for certain people, according
to their rejection or acceptance of him, either as a person or as
a writer. He fulminated in private letters and personal conversa-
tions against his critics, but he allowed the sharpest of these
antipathies free expression in public, calling his opponents by
name and besmirching their reputations with clever retorts.[18]
He frequently grouped all of his unfavorites together and pro-
ceeded to disparage their professional labor with the use of wit,

irony, satire, or sarcasm. Some of his best-known gibes, chosen at random from among his writings and interviews, are as follows:

The difference between the writer and the critic is that while the writer turns with anger on himself to bring satisfaction to his public, the critic directs his anger at others to satisfy himself.

Critics have frequently resisted the idea of attributing intelligence to me, but long ago I made up my mind to be intelligent without their permission.

Spanish critics have treated me unjustly, but then, when I first began writing, I treated them unjustly also, affirming that they had some talent.

Of all the spectators who fill a theater, it is usually the critic who demonstrates the least critical sense.

The critic is the author's parasite. His tools are incongruency, inanity, stupidity, discourtesy, and lies.

The critics, for their part, deployed their volleys with equally untiring devotion toward the crucifixion of Jardiel Poncela. Initially they were drawn into the fray by the playwright's presumptuous encroachment on their territory. In December of 1933, Jardiel published a critique on the contemporary theater scene, arrogating to himself the right and privilege to discuss at length the sad state of Spanish drama. This essay annoyed his adversaries because it condemns the prevailing mode of comedy in the 1920's and 30's with relentless scorn directed at many living writers, directors, and critics. Jardiel has words of praise only for the works of Martínez Sierra, Jacinto Benavente, the Quintero brothers, Carlos Arniches, García Álvarez, and Muñoz Seca, as well as a small number of playwrights of the poetic theater of his time (García Lorca, Eduardo Marquina, and José María Pemán). But he levels a blanket denunciation on all the rest, saying: "A multitude of mediocre writers remains, among them plagiarists and imitators; a veritable plague of theater sneak thieves, irresponsible people, devoid of artistic ability, and lacking the strength, therefore, to impel the theater public towards the ideal."[19]

Owing to the fact that this essay, a lively and humorous remonstrance against the mediocrity in his profession, centers its most caustic barbs on the practicing theater critics of Jardiel's time, all of them *madrileños*, Jardiel was thereafter considered an enemy of the billboard claque. The playwright attributes five capital defects to his critics, namely: a lack of enthusiasm for their work, personal vanity, absence of discernment, a destructive aim, and a deficiency of culture. There is little in this diatribe that would endear Jardiel Poncela to an insecure, threatened, or petty mind. Unquestionably, war was declared in December of 1933, with Jardiel hurling the first in a long series of unforgivable insults.

In all of his later prologues to individual plays or to play collections, Jardiel managed to convey a similar tone of malevolence towards his critics. These gentlemen often countered by a lack of praise for his artistry and of generosity in their comments on his plays. Some even ignored Jardiel's *estrenos*, or first-night performances, altogether. Others took him to task for his exuberance and his pride. Those who chose to review his premières, with the exception of Alfredo Marqueríe, who always praised Jardiel, did so briefly, conceding that his theater was simply too frivolous, too extravagant or too preposterous to be accorded serious critical attention.

Miguel Mihura disagrees with the popular notion that Jardiel's critics went after him for professional reasons. "It was his personality and person that invited their censure, not his theater," Mihura insists. "The attacks were made against his cynicism. He was vain, irritable, rancorous. He quarreled with everyone, especially as he gained success, but also when he needed money. The longer he lived, the more embittered he became."[20]

The conflict did not abate until Jardiel's death. His critics never forgave him his frank independence, and Jardiel could never overlook their petulance and deficiencies. The Spanish press generously eulogized him in 1952, but the residue of bitterness, an accumulation of twenty years of traumatic contention, remained to goad two of his surviving daughters, Mariluz and Evangelina, into writing several defenses for their father's position.[21]

Jardiel Poncela issued a valiant challenge to the rhetorical comic theater of his time, but his intent to rejuvenate Spanish comedy with daring departures from the ephemeral currents of popular farce was all too often garnished with sarcastic words of defiance at his critics and arrogant self-praise for his own accomplishments. Whatever success he enjoyed was the result of his talent, though the fundamental collapse of his higher intentions was largely the fault of an intransigent, proud strain in his personality that invited other proud but petty minds to deplore his egotistical peculiarities to such an extent that they failed to evaluate the singular importance of his theater. A large segment of the critical press never understood Jardiel. His wildly hyperbolic humor, his bold flights into fantasy and mystery, his uncompromising rejection of realism and verisimilitude remained totally beyond the grasp of his critics. And as long as Jardiel reacted emotionally to their adverse comments, the intellectual gap between them grew wider and wider.

IV   *Illness and Death*

Contradictory opinions still abound concerning Jardiel Poncela's lengthy illness and cause of death. In a recent series of interviews conducted in Madrid,[22] seven persons among twenty authors, actors, directors, and drama critics contacted stated emphatically that they believed Jardiel had gone insane. Six said he died of cancer, four of tuberculosis, four of nervous prostration, three of cardiac hypertrophy, two of pneumonia, and one declared suicide. His biographers, for what their suspect data is worth, seem just as confused. Canay contradicts himself in his careless monograph, opting for insanity, tuberculosis, cancer, and neurasthenia combined with the bitterness of melancholia, then shifting later in the same work to a belief that Jardiel died in full possession of his faculties following a long unnamed illness.[23] Flórez's strange statements about Jardiel's deathbed interview with a priest raised the ire of Evangelina Jardiel Poncela to such a point that she vigorously repudiates the Flórez biography as "a work of many falsehoods."[24]

Apparently, Jardiel himself did not know what ailed him. In 1950, one year before he died, he wrote that he had entered the New Year without youth or dreams, devoid of health and money, well into the sixth year of a mysterious affliction that even the doctors could not diagnose, "save that which only I know: that my life is draining away."[25]

Towards the end, Jardiel despised all medical practitioners. He refused their care, their advice, their recommendations. Upon refusing to take penicillin, he contracted pneumonia nine days before his death. It seems likely that, as Hammarstrand concludes, Jardiel's "nervous system, never too strong, had given way to the point of extreme neurasthenia."[26] And a major reason for his decline may also be Jardiel's recognition of his moral defeat, the result of an aggressive, neurotic reaction to ridicule and the sad realization that, if he was not to die completely friendless, he would indeed die quite alone.

CHAPTER 2

Plays of the Pre–War Era

FROM the time of his late adolescence to the outbreak of the Spanish Civil War in 1936, Jardiel Poncela wrote dozens of frivolous unpublished farces and staged eight major comedies. His early theater represented a departure from the norms, the concerns, and the objectives prevailing in Spanish stagecraft. With capricious starts and slumps, Jardiel labored to provide his spectators with a theater experience so singularly different, so daringly unlike anything they had ever witnessed or would ever see again, that his name, he believed, would become synonymous with notions of novelty, originality, and creative inventiveness in Spanish drama. Indeed, by the time he was thirty-five, when the Spanish Civil War erupted, most of Jardiel's writings had come to be valued or ridiculed solely on the basis of their dissimilarity from any conventional mode of comic or dramatic expression known to the theater audience of his day.

I Collaboration with Serafín Adame Martínez

Jardiel began his apprenticeship in the theater as an act of friendly collaboration with his upstairs neighbor, Serafín Adame Martínez. Time and differing opinions have obscured and perhaps exaggerated the exact number of complete full-length plays the two young men wrote together. José López Rubio affirms that before Jardiel was seventeen years old, the young playwright had written sixty-four theatrical pieces, most of them in partnership with Serafín Adame.[1] Alberto Canay states, but without documentation, that he is able to account for sixty works,[2] while Juan Bonet Gelabert provides us with the titles of only thirty-one plays written with Serafín Adame's aid.[3] Flórez reduces the listing to twenty-six named plays.[4] Jardiel himself often placed the number considerably higher. Any attempt to arrive at a correct and complete bibliography of Jardiel's youthful writings is futile, inasmuch as Jardiel repudiated all of his plays, short stories, and novels written before 1927 as "lamentable trash." Some of them he destroyed. Others he gave over to Serafín Adame in 1926, asking that they never be published bearing Jardiel's name. And still others are now condemned to perpetual oblivion under the jurisdiction of his daughter Evangelina. It was Jardiel's expressed wish that they never be examined, reproduced, published, or staged.

Surprisingly, though, eleven of his very early sketches were performed, some for a single staging. These included his first comedy of record, *Prince Raudhick* (*El príncipe Raudhick*), a four-act detective farce that he wrote with Serafín Adame for a short run in Bilbao in 1919. Jardiel and Serafín Adame were both seventeen at the time.

Serafín Adame was a fat, spoiled, myopic lad of fifteen when the two boys were first acquainted. They literally withdrew from the world together, spending long hours, night and day, absorbed in the flush and craze of youthful creativity.

There was no stopping our impetus. We began to tremble under the fever of an intensified production. Dramas, comedies, farces, zarzuelas, operettas, entremeses, monologues followed one upon the other.... We wrote because we had to, for the love of art, as a vocation.... We were somewhat stupid, but we were blessed with enthusiasm and good intentions.[5]

Serafín Adame went on to become a noted journalist and an obscure novelist and playwright. For several years he served as editor of the Madrid periodicals, *Informaciones* and *La Nación*. As it so often happened between the young author and his friends, a definitive rupture severed Jardiel's working relationship with his portly collaborator in 1926. At the time of the dissolution of their collaboration, Jardiel and Serafín Adame had a collection of forty-nine plays they were still revising.

The ten years of his collaboration with Serafín Adame enabled Jardiel to formulate in his mind a master plan for his future labors. At the age of twenty he had already determined, he writes, to elevate the quality of theatrical humor in Spain.[6]

This he would do by disclaiming all preceding attitudes by introducing novelty into his themes, and infusing dialogue with an originality of expression. His prolific and energetic activity with Serafín Adame had forged in his mind a clear resolution to begin a program of revolution in and for the theater. And he earnestly believed that, had it not been for the aggressive hostility of his critics, he would have been recognized in his time as one of this century's leading innovators of comic expression in playwriting.

II *First Stage Success:* A Sleepless Spring Night
(Una noche de primavera sin sueño)

Jardiel's so-called "first" production was actually, according to our closest tabulation, the sixty-fourth play he had written and the twelfth he had staged. The earlier writings he considered mere dabblings, a series of disconnected, superficial experiments worthy only of casual mention to demonstrate his love of the theater and to prove his allegiance to the discipline and craft of playwriting. When Jardiel declared that *A Sleepless Spring Night* betokened his legitimate debut as a dramatist, he was expressing as well his oft-repeated repudiation of everything he had written before that time.

Financial hardships prompted Jardiel to write *A Sleepless Spring Night*. His professional commitments were suffering under the pressure of extreme pecuniary reversals, a situation Jardiel labeled unbearable. In desperation he completed the first two acts after only four days of exhaustive labor, then turned over the incomplete manuscript to the noted actor Emilio Thuillier for his evaluation. Thuillier's response served to exalt and to injure the playwright's ego: The actor liked the play so much that he accused Jardiel of plagiarism, doubting that a work of such vigor and freshness could have originated from the mind of a young man of twenty-six years. Outraged by Thuillier's preposterous insinuation, Jardiel chose the most dramatic way of demonstrating his authorship: In the presence of the doubting Don Emilio, he ripped to shreds his newly-written third act which Thuillier had just read, then promised to write a new and better version within two days. Jardiel fulfilled his pledge and

Thuillier agreed to introduce him to the director of the Teatro Lara, Eduardo Yáñez, who in turn consented to stage the new comedy.

Several weeks of discomfiture and exasperation preceded the play's première of May 28, 1927. Yáñez, for Jardiel, did not take the play seriously enough. He delayed its performance, hoping that a work by a better-known writer would be commissioned in its place. A misunderstanding also erupted over a false report that Jacinto Benavente's private secretary had been directed by his employer to oppose all rehearsing of *A Sleepless Spring Night*. Reportedly, the eminent playwright and Nobel Prize winner insisted that no other play be prepared in the Lara as long as his own production, *Polichinela's Son* (*El hijo de Polichinela*), was being staged. Jardiel was again infuriated. He vowed to split Benavente's skull in half, but fortunately the erroneous report was rectified before any violence ensued.

The action of *A Sleepless Spring Night* begins during the concluding moments of an all-night dispute between Mariano and Alejandra, a young married couple. In anger, the husband leaves his apartment, only to be replaced by Valentín, a handsome stranger who enters through the open balcony window and spends the rest of the morning hours chatting with Alejandra. About noon, Mariano returns with his lawyer, intending to begin divorce proceedings. Learning of Valentín's presence, Mariano first accuses Alejandra of adultery, then threatens to kill her alleged lover. The young wife, convinced that her husband's display of jealous rage is proof of his love for her, turns her own wrath on the intruder for having contributed a possible motive for divorce action. In the end Valentín and Mariano reveal that they are old friends and had prearranged the entire episode of accusation and threatened homicide as a stratagem to enable the husband to win back Alejandra's affection. The confession of this ruse comes as a complete surprise both to Alejandra and the audience, and accounts for much of the play's effectiveness.

In the judgment of various critics, *A Sleepless Spring Night* constitutes "an outline of new intention,"[7] a work of incipient audacity which "sets the keynote for much of Jardiel's subsequent theater."[8] Alfredo Marqueríe calls attention to the rapid burlesque tone of the dialogue and the explosion of paradoxical situations. He affirms that the distinctive nature of Jardielesque humor, initiated by this play, "will be confirmed, ratified, and amplified in all the rest of the playwright's stage productions."[9]

The spectator's laughter does not spring forth by the effect of the clever arrangement of expressions in the sentence, but rather by what those expressions define and suggest; a concatenation of real contra-dictions which the spectator knows and has verified previously and which the character now summarizes ... as a complete and happy synthesis of something both justifiable and surprising.[10]

Marquerie is saying that here for the first time in Jardiel's lengthy theater experience we encounter the use of paradox and dialectic acrobatics applied both to situation and dialogue, that is, the accumulation of clever word games and involved situ-ations intended to confound and to amuse the audience. By way of unanticipated revelations and comic reversals, Jardiel leaves his spectators agonizing in bewilderment and laughter. Initially, the audience or reader experiences a nervous concern for the outcome of many apparently unfortunate happenings. One fears, for example, that the marriage covenant between Mariano and Alejandra is indeed endangered, that the wife might in fact become a party to adultery, that a murder of passion will perhaps result in conformity to that time-honored code which exacts punishment for suspected infidelity with an atoning flow of blood. However, these "typical" consequences never take place. Instead, Jardiel deploys familiar stage scenes in a very un-Spanish manner. As one example, the married couple discusses openly their marital problems with a candor quite unlike the un-communicative, reticent behavior we find so often depicted in the relationship between married people in the Spanish theater of Jardiel's time. The unexpected revelation of Valentín's true mission is likewise conveyed in an unconventional way, namely in a tone of light, sophisticated banter, in contrast to the more common denouements wherein problems are resolved in a cascading network of sobriety, aplomb, and dignity.

Alejandra's emancipated attitude denotes a new departure in a female protagonist: She is not molded after the long-suffering, faithful wife found in a Benavente heroine. The student of the liberated female in Spanish drama, who has customarily considered the heroines of Gregorio Martinez Sierra's theater to be the primary forerunners of the free-thinking, strong-willed woman of the modern-contemporary stage, would do well to reappraise the role, the impact, and the influence of Jardiel's Alejandra of 1927. She emerges as one of the most intelligent, articulate, and persuasive individuals of the twentieth-century Spanish theater. Her impassioned reproach of her husband's spiritual vulgarity, her charming control and cynicism in the presence of Valentín, and her overt rebellion against the routine, boring, and insipid commonplaces of everyday living, endear this creature to us as a vital symbol of liberation and independent thought.

Jardiel's play, for the year of its performance, was shocking, unorthodox, provocative, and quite original. His accumulation of exotic farcical tricks, his comic perversion of logic and congruity in the unstructured sequence of events, and his insistence on depicting character and rendering dialogue in an unconventional manner, confirm Marquerie's declaration that this work contains, in embryo and by implication, all of the characteristic values, "with all of the boldness, the inventions, and the audacities of content and form which make of Jardiel the innovator, the renovator, and the revolutionary of our comic genre."[11]

While Jardiel basked in the luxury of much positive acclaim for this play, he was also hounded by the first annoying mockery of his detractors. Unable to maintain his silence and equanimity when his attackers launched their gibes and jabs, Jardiel was soon recognized for his lack of resilience in the face of negative criticism. He singled out Enrique Díez-Canedo, for instance, for having "poisoned his happiness" with destructive comments.[12] Thereafter, the two men approached one another with strained civility, bordering on quiet rage, in public, but allowed their mutual hostility to erupt in print following each new première of a Jardiel play. Theirs was an unrelieved hostility, beginning with Enrique Jardiel Poncela's first major play and ending only with the playwright's death.

III *Five Early Farces*

"Jardielism" emerged with unsteady starts and cautious plodding. The revolutionary boldness of *A Sleepless Spring Night* may have aroused Marquerie's devoted attachment to Jardiel's innovative manner, but one admirer's fervid allegiance did little to convert critical regard into commercial distinction. Jardiel learned early that his public valued concession and compromise much higher than it did the unfettered expression of novelty. If any pattern can be ascribed to his efforts to write in a unique and original way, it would have to be stated in econo-gastronomic terms: Whenever he was well off and well fed, Jardiel allowed his artistic impulses to run wild, but during those grim periods of near starvation, he curbed his passion for inventiveness and shunned diversity in order to cultivate the type of conventional drama he found most contemptible in other playwrights. Five of his early farces attest to this trial of conscience, to the uneven give and take between the unique outburst of Jardielesque humor and the controlled tempering of his craft. Jardiel would live to know more wretched days than those he spent attempting to weigh and assess the public's reaction to his first set of plays, but he never afterwards suffered from that unsavory awareness of self-deception. His writings at this early time reveal the personal displeasure that comes to one in the wake of the prostitution of his artistic ideals. Later, when he was financially secure, Jardiel was hated by multitudes and he hated them in return, yet he enjoyed a sense of knowing that he was true to his own understanding of the world.

A. *A Jardielesque Monstrosity*: Señor García's Cadaver
   (El cadáver del Señor García)

While still in his late twenties, Jardiel began to experience periods of doleful self-effacement. Only by sudden bursts of creative energy could he extricate himself from those sinister clouds of gloom. He knew few moments of discontent so pervasive as the ennui which preceded the writing of *Señor García's Cadaver,* or the utter dispondency he suffered following the play's monumental failure.

Jardiel was compelled to write *Señor García's Cadaver* as a frenzied effort to dispel tension, depression, and irritability. Over two years had passed since he had enjoyed the singular success of *A Sleepless Spring Night;* the play had triumphed in terms of its box-office receipts, which Jardiel had long since squandered, but it had failed to give him the kind of prominence and glory he was anticipating. During the interim he wrote only two comedies, *The Ten Forty-five Express* (*El rápido de las 10 y 45*) and *Madame Delfos,* but both were rejected by the impresario who had commissioned them, and then the manuscript to each was subsequently lost during a short change of residence. Jardiel's sense of defeat was exacerbated by the incisive reminders from the café crowd that he was a "one-play, one-success" writer. He had to prove himself, to convince his friends that his first triumph was not an accident. With that unusual abruptness with which he characteristically ended his fits of despair, Jardiel plunged into writing the first act of a new farce. As he had done in writing *A Sleepless Spring Night,* he completed Act One in less than two days. Before commencing the final act, he took the manuscript to Casimiro Ortas, the first actor of the Teatro Comedia, who in turn introduced the play and its author to the theater company's director, Tirso Escudero. Within five weeks, while the play was being rehearsed, Jardiel wrote the remainder of *Señor García's Cadaver.* By mid-February, only two months following his initial haste to write as a panacea for melancholia, the play was performed on the stage of one of Madrid's most prestigious theaters.

This three-act farce is, by its own merits, neither as bad as the critics proclaimed, nor as good as Jardiel aspired to make it, yet certain aspects of its confusing plot and its unkind reception warrant our attention; indeed, it is at this important juncture in the playwright's career, owing to the negative impact of one mediocre play, that Madrid's comic theater world was split into two discordant camps, namely: those few who never flagged in their support of Jardiel's outlandish escapades, and the many who voiced a deep-seated aversion for everything he would thereafter undertake. In the words of one of his later admirers, the decisive collapse of *Señor García's Cadaver* divided the theatergoing public into *jardielistas* and *antijardielistas*.[13]

The play concerns the apparent suicide, because of unrequited love, of Señor García, a man who, shortly before entering the darkened room of the apartment he supposes belongs to his girlfriend, had learned of the young lady's intention to marry another. A sound from the street of several tires blowing out has caused Señor García to faint, thus leading both the spectators and the wedding guests who discover his "corpse" to suspect a suicide. A note is found in his coat pocket attesting to the fact that the bride-to-be had abandoned him and had thus caused his death. The real groom indignantly repudiates his betrothed, but then it turns out that Señor García had mistakenly entered the wrong apartment, interrupting a different wedding celebration. Other equivocal situations follow, such as the disclosure that García's true sweetheart has borne him a child, a fact which leads to another faked suicide. The play is a hodgepodge of exaggerated surprises, conducting the spectator from a simple network of amusing entanglements in Act One to the most bewildering maze of absurdities in Acts Two and Three. Unfortunately, the progressively farcical mood of the comedy carries the audience from an improbable situation which seems to promise the execution of an impressive artistic success, to the proliferation of such juvenile burlesque as to destroy the imaginative warmth of the early promise. The play ends happily for the protagonist and his newfound friends, but it left Jardiel's public stamping its feet in anger and screaming its protest.

If the spectators' message was not made clear, the critics who attacked the comedy for its "progressive violence and contumacy" against all logic and sobriety of purpose endorsed the play's rapid demise. It was removed from the stage following its seventh performance, which played to an almost empty house.

For the most part, the audience had been offended by Jardiel's irreverence towards the theme of death. When García's body is found, for instance, the neighbors are not depicted with any display of concern, compassion, or fear, but only with an eagerness to find some new excitement that might enable them to dispel their boredom. The critics, for their part, claimed that Jardiel abused all sense of propriety, accumulating comic devices to such an extreme that he finally exasperated his spectators. It is "an impossible play," wrote one commentator, "and not only impossible, but bad, absolutely beneath the talents of its author, full of comic scenes that are frankly irritating."[14]

Jardiel disagreed. He diagnosed his error as a hesitancy to continue the progressive assemblage of exaggerated situations beyond the first act.[15] While conceding that *Señor García's Cadaver* was his greatest commercial failure,[16] he insisted that had the extremes been accentuated rather than reduced, he would have had a clamorous success.[17]

"They despise me," Jardiel wrote a month after the play closed, "they consider me washed up, a failure, before I've even begun. But if their pleasure depends upon their seeing me saddened and disheartened, then their pleasure has ended from this moment on."[18] Such was Jardiel's warcry, his first public announcement that a long and brutal battle with his critics was beginning. And such was his stubborn refusal to give in, to change his dramatic posture, to forsake his search for that inimitable form of comic expression which unfortunately had its first major appearance in a coarse and clumsy play teeming with such disparate and unexpected trickery as to alienate a good part of his audience. Some have never to this day forgiven the playwright the extravagances of that early indulgence in comic intemperance.

Despite his professed intent to avoid discouragement, Jardiel sagged into a desperate mood of bitterness and self-mortification. For several months his lack of confidence tended to persuade him to forsake the theater altogether. It was only through the encouragement of his new friend, Tirso Escudero, the same impresario who had taken a chance with a public staging of *Señor García's Cadaver,* that Jardiel Poncela returned to the theater in 1931 with another production, one conceived in every way to please the public and to invite critical acclaim.

B. *A Play of Decorum*: Margarita, Armando and His Father
    (Margarita, Armando y su padre)

The storm of protest which had occasioned the failure of
Señor García's Cadaver left Jardiel as financially encumbered
as he was emotionally drained. His return to playwriting, out
of deference to Tirso Escudero's wishes, compelled him to
discard audacity for the practical demands of subsistence.
Fearing also the utter collapse of his literary career if he
failed again, Jardiel pledged to himself that his third play
would be a commercial and critical triumph. But to bring off
such a feat would oblige him to exercise the same kind of
craft he despised in so many writers; he would have to prostitute
his inventive flair, diminish his absurdist trend, and forego
innovative purposes. The result was *Margarita, Armando and
His Father,* a modern adaptation and parody of Alexandre
Dumas' romantic drama, *La Dame aux camélias* (1852).

In four acts, Jardiel develops a logical and well-controlled
plot filled with the cabaret spirit of the pre-Republic period
of Spain. His two main characters, Armando and Margarita,
are struck by the similarity of their amorous relationship with
that of Armand Duval and Marguerite Gautier in Dumas'
celebrated work. But quite unlike the ingenuous character of
Georges Duval, *père,* Armando's colorful and crafty father
willingly encourages the affair, even to the point of contributing
a large monthly allowance to perpetuate the young couple's
idyllic alliance. He is secretly opposed to the match, however,
and brings about its dissolution by repeated acts of kindness.
Knowing that comforts reduce passion, that the removal of
obstacles contributes to domestic weariness, he enables Margarita to keep her jewels and helps Armando to avoid
employment. The inevitable result of the couple's induced
prosperity and idleness is their realization that they are utterly
bored with one another and they voluntarily agree to separate.

The play has a dash of the characteristic wit and cynicism
of Jardiel's best writings, but it is so thoroughly conventional,
so mechanically efficient *a la Scribe* that Jardiel himself
labeled it "a facile, insincere comedy."[19] It stands as the least
representative of his repertory. It did succeed, nonetheless, in

bringing the playwright enormous economic returns for his effort, in that the production was labeled a magnificent work by most of Madrid's undiscerning critics.[20]

While time has not confirmed the validity of the play's early success, it should be pointed out, in fairness to Jardiel's earnest attempt to salvage a sense of good literary taste from a work of dry, prescriptive decorum, that the last act, a kind of epilogue in which the lovers are briefly reunited long after their definitive separation, is indeed well written. Jardiel had completed the first three acts within one month's time, thinking of his public throughout the creative process. It was only after consulting with Milagros Leal, the distinguished actress who played the role of Margarita, that Jardiel determined to write the fourth act to please only himself. In so doing, he chose to ruin Margarita's happiness, departing from Dumas' story line, but this one Jardielesque feature imbued the play with its only concrete evidence of sincerity. Bonet has called the ending "the finest, deepest and most delicious moment of the entire comedy."[21]

C. *Wealth Bred of Mediocrity*: You Have the Eyes of a Fatal Woman (*Usted tiene los ojos de mujer fatal*)

Jardiel's fourth play appeared to be ill-fated from its inception. He rewrote its short prologue eighteen times over a five-month period. Then his daughter Evangelina contracted bronchial pneumonia, forcing a lengthy delay in the completion of the first act, Jardiel blustered and worried over the problem of suiting the comedy's action to the role of a particular actress, and he struggled repeatedly with the difficult task of converting the plot of his long novel, *Eleven Thousand Virgins*, into a theatrical work. Added to these pains of composition, Jardiel found himself arbitrating a lengthy personal feud between his leading lady and a jealous, infuriated Milagros Leal, to whom he had assigned a demeaning secondary part. Moreover, the play was scheduled to follow the closing of *La OCA*, a successful comedy by Muñoz Seca and Pérez Fernández, which ran the entire theater season and therefore obliged Jardiel to postpone his play's première for another year.

In the end, the director rejected Jardiel's work, refused to have it staged, and offered the playwright no remuneration for his lost time and labor. Some of Jardiel's associates even declined to read the condemned play, and one who did read it called it unperformable. Predictably, Jardiel abandoned the theater with a proud, scornful shrug and retreated into his shell of depression. His emotional agitation was short-lived, however, with the offer of a six-month filming contract from a friend in Hollywood. So, with little concern for the fate of his unstaged play, Jardiel turned it over to an actor, packed his bags, and left for California. During Jardiel's absence, Benito Cibrián, the actor in question, directed the first performance of *You Have the Eyes of a Fatal Woman* in Valencia, in spite of the playwright's own prediction that the production was predestined to suffer a resounding failure. When Jardiel returned to Spain, his play had already been staged in five of Madrid's leading theaters, having surpassed 350 performances. Before the year ended, this "unperformable" work established a new national record by being performed over one thousand times throughout the nation.[22] Jardiel's financial gains were large, and his name and fame were solidly confirmed.

The comedy, consisting of a prologue and three acts, is a simplified version of Jardiel's third novel, *Eleven Thousand Virgins,* complete with all of the long narrative's misogynist trappings.[23] It concerns the amorous exploits of Sergio Hernán, a modern Don Juan whose reputation has attracted the attention of a group of would-be heirs to another man's fortune. As the millionaire's fiancée represents a threat to their inheritance, they employ Don Sergio to seduce the girl and thus lead her away from their victim. By fatal chance, the girl turns out to be the one conquest with whom Sergio had fallen in love some years earlier. She discovers that Sergio is courting her for a price and leaves him. For a time Sergio wallows in self-pity and despair, but his melancholy serves to convince the girl of his sincerity and love. She returns to him, and the play ends on the theme of the unconquerable lover reconquered.

Notwithstanding its great commercial success, the play offers little innovative or literary merit. Even Rafael Flórez, Jardiel's most adoring apologist, admits to the play's artistic weakness.[24]

It follows the same coherent, nonaudacious pattern of Jardiel's *Margarita, Armando and His Father*. The situation in which the protagonist becomes embroiled with his former sweetheart, and the revelation to the audience of his amorous techniques, are the primary attractions of the play. It is clever, witty, entertaining, but virtually devoid of the titillating and controversial "Jardielesque" flavor that permeates the author's later writings. Obviously, it was written to mollify Jardiel's critics and to fatten his bank account.

D. *Cynicism in a Hurry*: A Proper Adultery
   (Un adulterio decente)

Jardiel began writing *A Proper Adultery* aboard the ocean liner that returned him to Spain from his second journey to the United States in March of 1935. Upon his arrival in Madrid, he was informed that a play was urgently needed within a few weeks for the traditional opening of the spring theater season. Jardiel complied by completing, within twenty days, the amusing and skillfully written first act of *A Proper Adultery*. But he encountered extreme difficulty maintaining the same high tone, quality, and direction in writing the remaining two acts. So convinced was Jardiel that his hastily conceived play was doomed to failure, that he withdrew it for further revisions the same day of its scheduled première performance. He promised his chagrined theater company to have the work completely revised and back in their hands in less than a week. But the precipitation with which the final acts had to be rewritten, together with the last-minute substitution of an actor for the lead role, imposed such demands on Jardiel that his determination, energy, and creative genius were not adequate to vitalize a work of uneven texture. He managed to turn out a tolerably good play, but the last two acts remained dreadfully artificial by comparison to the brilliant opening.

A Proper Adultery exemplifies Jardiel's unorthodox approach to conventional morality. He depicts the unusual situation of a wife's having invented an imaginary husband to replace her own spouse, Eduardo, when the latter goes out of town. The fictitious husband exists only in her mind as the executor of a

proper and decent form of adultery. She does in truth have
another lover—his name is Federico—but as long as she
believes she is cheating with a make-believe man, her true
husband, she imagines, is not going to be hurt. Eduardo,
however, happens to return unexpectedly, only to encounter
Federico in his living room. Federico has been led to believe
that Eduardo is merely a very dear friend of the family. To
Federico's effusive greeting, Eduardo reacts with utter bewilderment, an emotion surpassed only by Federico's astonishment
upon learning of Eduardo's true marital relationship. The first
act ends at the height of the two men's extreme consternation.

In Act Two Jardiel introduces his principal character in
the person of Dr. Cumberri, a comic individual who suffers
constant distractions and lapses of memory. The doctor has set
up an asylum for the cure of adulterous wives. It is his
contention that adultery is caused by a bacillus, and thus he
prescribes as a cure for Eduardo's wife a term of isolation
until the patient falls in love with her husband again. In this
case, though, the wife still loves her husband, so the doctor
must decide on a different course of action. He prescribes
locking up the adulterous lovers, apart from Eduardo, to allow
familiarity to generate contempt and time to bring about the
inevitable boredom, and thus dissolve their amorous feelings
for one another. The plan succeeds, and once again a play ends
underlining Jardiel's cynical attitude towards love and marriage.

The extravagant behavior of each individual in the triangle,
compounded by Dr. Cumberri's strange methods for curing
adultery, falls within the best currents of Jardielesque humor.
The play's farcical tendencies, however, reduce the incontest-
ably high tone of humor in Act One to low-level slapstick in
the last two acts. This gives the impression, as Phyllis Z.
Boring states, "of a completely artificial appendage to fill out
a three-act format."[25]

The clownish character of Dr. Cumberri fits well within the
literary tradition of medical eccentrics, from the quacks of
Latin comedy through Molière's brutal charlatans to Casona's
amiable Dr. Ariel. But Cumberri does more to cheapen the
play's initial tone of sophisticated humor than any other farcical
element in Jardiel's work. Indeed, the playwright's shift in

Act Two from a dramatic focus on the wife's peculiar dilemma to a caricature of the medical specialist destroys whatever unity of action the play seemed to promise. Díez-Canedo is correct in his conjecture that had Jardiel continued to feature the wife as the protagonist, the play might well have become a tragicomedy of Pirandellian proportions.[26]

E. *A Casual Courtship with a Traditional Yarn*:
Satan's Five Warnings (Las cinco advertencias de Satanás)

During his second residence in Hollywood, Jardiel determined to write a play based on the Devil's personal visitation to a notorious Don Juan figure. He developed the details and began writing the first act while recuperating from a bout with typhoid fever in the summer of 1935. Paying strict attention to his own criteria for assuring a rigorous unity of action within the context of an improbable dialogue and fantastic occurrences, he completed the play's four acts by October 5 of the same year. In the end, however, his intended director, Eduardo Yáñez of Madrid's Teatro Lara, declined to stage the work, giving as his reason a preference to première a new play by Carlos Arniches, the aging master of the *sainete*. In actuality, the Lara company had gone bankrupt: by April of 1936 the theater was obliged to close its doors. Jardiel eventually sought the assistance of his trusted friend, Tirso Escudero, who consented to underwrite the play's staging in the Teatro Comedia on December 20, 1935.

In addition to his having enveloped the plot with an unusual display of humorous wordplay, Jardiel sustains the spectator's interest with the gradual revelation of five diabolic predictions which affect the mortal life style of his wealthy but aging and disillusioned protagonist, Don Félix. Félix has misspent his mature years in a futile search for happiness. In desperation, he has flitted from one illicit love affair to another, like a man fearful that old age will soon find him incapable of amorous experiences. He is on the brink of renouncing all women forever when the Devil appears to him and foretells the imminence of four soul-stirring happenings, the fourth of which will be preceded by the pronouncement of an inevitable fifth admonition, which Satan defines as the most terrible and painful revelation of all, and as such it must remain a secret to Don Félix and to the audience until the first four events have transpired.

The Devil's first admonition is that Félix be prepared for meeting a beautiful, charming, seductive woman. The second warning concerns the probability that Félix will fall madly in love with this mysterious female. The third matter of satanical advice warns Félix that she will likely fall in love with him. And the fourth—a fearful calamity—alerts Félix to the fact that when they are both at the height of their romantic pleasure, he will be forced, by the knowledge he will receive as his fifth warning, to relinquish her to the arms of his rival.

Jardiel carefully manipulates the first three acts to disclose the working out of the first three events, in spite of the protagonist's rash efforts to disown his fate and to forestall any occurrence of the fourth and fifth warnings. Félix's disbelief in Satan's power compels him to resist falling into the trap of a predestined alliance with the mysterious female, but once he finds himself hopelessly ensnarled in the romance, he is lost to her wiles and she to his charms. In the end, following three months of courtship and just short of consummating their mounting attachment for one another, Félix discovers the awful truth in the Devil's fifth pronouncement: that the woman is, in reality, Félix's own daughter, the fruit of an old forgotten love affair. Horrified that he is faced with the choice of abandoning her or engaging in an incestuous relationship, he chooses to renounce the woman, and she, as so many of Félix's hapless lovers before her, flees to the arms of his rival.

Satan's Five Warnings, which Marqueríe labels a first-rate "comedy of impossible love,"[27] provides Jardiel with multiple opportunities to express his misogynist feelings with statements reminiscent of those flashes of antifeminist virulence we find in his four novels and in such plays as *A Proper Adultery.* He employs a personal touch of contrariness with the unveiling of each prophesied event, applying to his dialogue many amusing verbal twists and clever paradoxical retorts, aimed principally at women. This semantic funfare is a typical Jardielesque principle which some critics have praised as an ingenious manifestation of "the false relation of causality,"[28] while others, less prone to assign any positive value to such tendencies, regard it as an aberration of the comic spirit which dehumanizes the natural flow of humor.[29]

Throughout his play, Jardiel toys with producing two distinct and contrary effects in the spectator's mind, achieved primarily by the exercise of puns, quips, witticisms, and incongruous remarks. Félix's vain efforts to curb the design of the inevitable also allows Jardiel to manipulate his protagonist's words along one line of reasoning, that being an affirmation of resistance to fate, while the spectator is made aware of the fact that the hero's own past record of licentious conduct determines a different course for his life. In the final scenes, Félix confronts not the censure of a supernatural judgment, but the simple consequences of his own imprudent acts. Despite the comic trappings and the presence of fantasy in this play, represented by Jardiel's having revived the age-old theme of the Devil's involvement in human concerns, conmingled with the traditional Don Juan figure's proud disdain before the future consequences of his past behavior, the work conveys an ostensible existential message that a man's life is the product of his own choices. Perhaps these attributes account for Rafael Flórez's high estimation of this play[30] and the recorded judgment of Gregorio Martínez Sierra, one of Jardiel's close associates and a distinguished playwright in his own right, that *Satan's Five Warnings* is among the best comedies Jardiel had written, "a complete, delightful, and admirable play."[31] Had Jardiel taken his subject more seriously, discarding his frequent concessions to cheap comedy and replacing the froth with a dimension of metaphysical concern for his hero's dilemma, he may well have produced a work of enduring literary and philosophical persuasion.

IV *Two Important Comedies*

Jardiel's material success, despite his inclination to squander his income, enabled him to give free rein to his own inventive capacities and idiosyncrasies to resolve the enormous technical problems inherent in the structuring of his uncommon, extravagant plays. He categorically refused to make the concessions demanded of him by his earlier indigent circumstances. In two prewar comedies he reaches that plane of self-reliant maturity he had been aiming at since his days of collaboration with Serafín Adame Martínez, namely, to devise a theater whose mechanics of comicity would be based from beginning to end on the idea of inverisimilitude, incongruity, and unrestrained originality. This marked the authentic debut of a consistent ground swell of Jardielism.

A. *A Well-Balanced Parody*: Angelina, or a Brigadier's Honor
(Angelina, o El honor de un brigadier)

Angelina is a parody in verse of nineteenth-century melodrama. Its humor results from a use of caricature to exaggerate the frills, costumes, customs, and stereotypes of the post-Romantic theater of José Echegaray and his disciples. Jardiel imitates the poetic style of the period he is satirizing by employing an easy, prosaic type of verse—octosyllables with consonantal rhyme. The end rhyme, coupled with the vivacity and cleverness of the language and rhythm, results in substantial comic dividends.

Before he began writing this play, the author studied the dramatic techniques of several late nineteenth-century playwrights and researched the customs and feelings of the time. Two plays particularly impressed him as containing most of the elements he desired to parody, namely *The Gordian Knot* (*El nudo gordiano*) of Eugenio Sellés, which in its heyday (1878) was staged many hundreds of times and received the plaudits of those who were stirred by the exalted clamor and madness of thesis plays; and *The Passion Flower* (*La pasionaria*) of Leopoldo Cano, whose versified histrionics, best exemplified by this play (1883), contributed no small increment to the neo-Romantic school of Echegaray.

Jardiel's play, set in the year 1880, deals with a man's concern for his honor. In the prologue each character introduces himself and indicates the nature of the role he will play. The hero, heroine, and villain are clearly defined by their noble, kind, or evil intentions. The story line is quite simple, but predictably implausible: Angelina, the daughter of Don Marcial, the brigadier general of the play's subtitle, elopes with Germán on the very day of her engagement to Rodolfo, a young poet who travels about on a bicycle. Don Marcial's honor has been offended by this impertinent act, so he and the jilted cyclist go in pursuit of the wayward lovers. Discovering his daughter's seducer at long last, Don Marcial challenges Germán to a duel. In the heat of combat, Marcial learns that his own wife, Marcela, has also betrayed him, and with none other than the same intemperate rogue who ran away with his daughter and who stands in mortal peril before him. All of the characters plead with Don Marcial to spare Germán and to forgive the dishonored Marcela, just as Rodolfo has consented to do with Angelina. Confused, enraged, but doubting his own powers of judgment, Don Marcial invokes the spirit of his departed father for some wise supernatural guidance. The ghost appears and persuades Don Marcial to pardon his spouse. Marcial agrees, but only on the condition that his rival die. Germán thereby agrees to leave the country, intent upon fighting to his death for a remote cause in a distant war. And thus ends this three-act burlesque which mocks the ideal of honor, satirizes the notion of sacrifice for a noble cause, and spoofs without acrimony many bygone theatrical mannerisms.

The play is a composite of hilarious incidents, sentimental affairs, cynical nonsense, and freewheeling extravagance. "Dramatically a perfect work," claims Rafael Flórez, who ranks *Angelina* as one of Jardiel's four best productions.[32] "As perishable as the timeworn dramas it parodies," declares Díez-Canedo, again reminding us that not all critics would agree with respect to Jardiel's worth.[33] Nevertheless, at least one major writer of the time was so favorably impressed with *Angelina* that he dedicated a series of three journalistic glosses to extol its merits. That writer was the famous Catalonian essayist and art critic, Eugenio d'Ors (1882–1954), who invited his readers of the Madrid newspaper *El Debate* to examine the original thought-provoking notions and the unusual humor underlying Jardiel's lively parody.[34] Some twelve years later, d'Ors modified his opinion of Jardiel and put in question his role as a reformer, calling him instead "an eccentric of theater literature" who passed each day as if he were hallucinating.[35] The earlier judgment, however, prevailed in Jardiel's mind much longer than the latter; the playwright often cited d'Ors's complimentary words to defend his innovative manner and to put down his enemies.

The importance of *Angelina* stems from the elegance and grace of its poetic form and the good-humored tone of its content. It is a finished piece of writing, providing the reader with one of those rare moments in Jardiel Poncela: an encounter with a play which is balanced in all three acts, perfected in all scenes, faultless in every speech and rejoinder. It is to Jardiel's credit that before submitting the completed manuscript to Arturo Serrano of the Infanta Isabel Theater, he sought after and accepted the advice of two accomplished playwrights, Eduardo Marquina and Gregorio Martínez Sierra.[36] Their candid criticism of the work contributed to the formation of *Angelina* as a play of solid literary quality, with no loss of evenness or spontaneity.

B. *The Exceptional Fantasy:*
    Four Hearts in Check and Backward March
    (Cuatro corazones con freno y marcha atrás)

Jardiel believed that his comedies, *Four Hearts in Check and Backward March* and *A Round-Trip Husband* were the two best plays he had ever written. He rejoiced in their improbability and esteemed the imaginative fantasy and comic extravagance of their plots far above the best qualities of his previous and later writings. In the more than twenty years since Jardiel's death, critical opinion has tended to vindicate the playwright's personal judgment. Francisco Ruiz Ramón agrees that each work represents for its time the culmination of Jardiel's artistic passion for the absurd: *Four Hearts* as his prewar masterpiece, and *A Round-Trip Husband* as his most significant play of the post-Civil War period.[37] Francisco García Pavón also sets apart these two titles from Jardiel's impressive repertory as being the best exponents of the author's "vigorous talents and capacity of invention."[38] Jardiel was so proud of his achievement in writing *Four Hearts in Check and Backward March*, that he immodestly announced to his public, in advance of the comedy's première, that it was "an exceptional work in its genre, nurtured by fantasy, upheld by the strength of ingenuity and incidental richness, and of such a high quality with respect to the rest of the contemporary scene's comic production that, without stooping to insult, it admits no comparison nor possible sequel."[39]

The author's affinity for *Four Hearts* stems in large measure from the work's lengthy gestation. The first act, which he wrote while vacationing in Tablada, dates back to 1926. It was not until 1931 that a newly revised version of this act was offered to the humorist K-Hito for publication in *Gutiérrez*. Four years later, Jardiel began the second act and again rewrote the revised version of the first act. Finally, under contact in 1936 to deliver the entire play for a May première, ten years after it was first conceived, Jardiel managed to complete the difficult third act. He experienced, in fact, such ardor and frustration in finishing the play that he felt compelled to make a special pilgrimage to his mother's tomb in Quinto del Ebro where, searching desperately for inspiration, he derived the necessary strength to write Act Three in only five days.

The play was first staged under a different title: *Dying Is a Mistake* (*Morirse es un error*). It was enjoying an extraordinary run at Madrid's Infanta Isabel Theater when, in July of 1936, the Spanish Civil War erupted. Three years later, when peace was restored, so was Jardiel's play. With its return to the stage, the title was changed in view of its inopportune reference to death. Thus Jardiel's most preferred work completed a record performance some thirteen years after the composition of its first act.

The plot concerns the discovery in 1860 of a marvelous saline solution extracted from algae which stops the aging process in tissue and thus assures perpetual youth or immortality. The discoverer, Dr. Bremón, invites a group of friends to join him to prolong their mortal existence indefinitely. Each of the principals consents to the experiment for selfish and personal reasons—to perpetuate physical beauty, love, and wealth. Their exhilaration and optimism while pursuing an uninterrupted state of bliss are the focus of Act One. The second act takes place in the year 1920, sixty years later. We now find the privileged immortals in a state of forlorn misery and ennui, self-exiled to a remote desert island. They have withdrawn from the rest of the human race, owing to the terrible tedium of changelessness. The jarring contact with normal mortal concerns is too hard for them to bear. Life has lost meaning and pleasure now that there is no end in sight. The bliss with which they contemplated perpetual youth has turned sour, and their days are filled with contention, recrimination, and grief. For religious reasons they must reject the thought of suicide.

The solution to their problem is worked out in Act Three. Moving ahead in time another sixteen years, the isolated immortals learn that Dr. Bremón has discovered yet another miracle drug, a similar saline distillation that will make them progressively younger until they return to the moment of birth and then . . . disappear! Each individual accepts this option with glee, recognizing that by reversing the chronology of his life, he can once again infuse his existence with a meaningful pattern and goal. This inversion of the natural order, however, affects an equal distortion upon the social and moral orders. The subjects' children and grandchildren are now obliged to care for their irresponsible parents, who have passed one hundred years of age, yet act more and more like adolescents. One of the youthful elders falls in love with his grandmother-in-law because she is the only one who understands him. And Valentina, now 105 years old, fears the day will come when she will be younger than the child she is expecting! Bickering breaks out anew as Dr. Bremón's childlike disciples contend incessantly with their relatives. The play ends without a clear resolution for their predicament: Each companion awaits the certain oblivion that will follow his infancy.

Jardiel might have achieved a work of solid metaphysical importance had he not allowed the light tone of his dialogue and the surge of his playful puns—often structured around such notions as eternity, birth, and death—to prevail over the significant message that underlies the play's farcical mood. Once again verbal clowning and frivolous events take precedence over any kind of stimulating philosophical ideology. The levity Jardiel deploys is so pervasive as to obviate our taking the work seriously. However, as we consider the content and impact of this play, we must remind ourselves that Jardiel is not in the least preoccupied with social, moral, political, or philosophical matters. He is not a man of ideas, but of superficial amusements. He deliberately reduces an important problem to a level of non-sense and triviality, stripping thought of its intellectual challenge to supplant it with easy laughter. The theater exigencies of his day paid him to do this, and he fulfilled that commitment better than most playwrights of his generation. Nevertheless, in *Four Hearts in Check and Backward March*, despite his refusal to approach any serious problem with honesty and depth, Jardiel comes closer than in any other play he authored to endowing his work with a dash of bold, ponderable substance. The reader or spectator will still come away from this comedy asking himself several provocative questions, such as: What will happen when people have all the time they can wish for?; or what would occur if we were to find a formula for everlasting life on earth and boredom finally overcame us?; or again, how does it feel to want nothing after everything in the realm of one's immediate interest has been attained? Jardiel appears to proffer some answers, but even these remain unsatisfactory for a serious mind. Whatever important problems might have surfaced are too often reduced or avoided by the author's air of casual, sometimes snickering skepticism.

CHAPTER 3

Plays of the Post–War Era

JARDIEL Poncela's post-Spanish Civil War writings are characterized by original experimentations. Initially, they are works of a consummate technical skill, impressive for their controlled structure and the incremental swell of humorous incidents, but unsettling as well for their heavy dependency on complex subplots and puzzling intrigue. In their final phase, the comedies become, owing to Jardiel's massive stress on originality, veritable miscreations of comic eccentricity. The socalled humor of Jardielism knows no moment of restraint from 1939 to 1949, but its flame of extremism is constantly operative. At its best, with *Heloise Lies Under an Almond Tree*, Jardielism is unassailably dazzling, titillating, and exhilarating; at its worst, with *Tigers Hidden in the Bedroom*, Jardielism is a kind of pathetic aberration, a funny dream that is suddenly inhabited by monsters.

I *The Apex of Jardielism:*
Heloise Lies Under An Almond Tree
(Eloísa está debajo de un almendro)

Heloise is a play of bewildering, sophisticated madness. It consists of a long delightful prologue that has nothing whatever to do with the two acts which follow; a plot of great complexity that has relatively little to do with the play's popularity; no less than thirty characters, few of whom have any affiliation with rational behavior; and a staggering conglomeration of hilarious scenes which have no connection with the norms and premises of conventional humor. *Heloise*, to be savored, must be viewed or read to be appreciated; for one who lacks a personal acquaintance with the play, only the broad surface mechanics of its construction can be apprehended. Indeed, the proliferation and intricacy of its comic devices defy our rendering a really satisfactory summary of the plot. The full force of its hysteria-producing properties can only best be transmitted by a worthy stage production. Following a good performance of *Heloise*, the spectator will emerge from the theater—as was our experience after viewing a *reposición* at Madrid's María Guerrero Theater on Christmas Eve of 1964—in a limp and laugh-weary stupor, the victim of a calculated contagion of convulsive mirth. This is, of course, all Jardiel intended: to infuse his dialogue and comic situations with an uninterrupted series of brilliant verbal surprises, paradox, irony, and puns, designed to provoke laughter without recourse to topical jokes, slapstick, or trite, timeworn gimmicks.

The highly regarded prologue to *Heloise* is a veritable *entremés*, an independent vignette of Madrilenean *costumbrismo*. Its action takes place in the last row of a *barrio* movie house where some nineteen moviegoers plus an usher face the audience in anticipation of the beginning of a film. Their antics, quips, repartee, and rejoinders serve to prepare our minds for the dazzling absurdities to follow, although in substance the prologue is unrelated to the later plot development. Juan Emilio Aragonés cites the prologue as an example of Jardiel's tendency to create isolated complications and to accumulate mischievous subplots "as a simple diversion to prove to everyone his astounding capacity for resolving them and even, if he feels so disposed, for demonstrating that they have a relevant meaning."[1] In this case, however, it appears that Jardiel is merely teasing his spectators; the lengthy episode in the movie house has no "relevant meaning" other than to entertain us for its own sake.

Many strange people say and do many strange things throughout the two long acts of this strange comedy. Perhaps the strangest creature of them all is Edgardo Briones, who has spent over twenty years in bed listening to the radio, shooting his gun to test the nervous disposition of new maids, and pretending to travel every evening on a locomotive. His behavior conveys the greatest dramatic impact with a strong tinge of pathos, since it is the result of his having witnessed, several years before, the murder of his wife Heloise at the hands of his demented sister

Micaela, whom he now protects by his own feigned madness in order to avoid sending her to an institution. He himself had buried Heloise in the garden under an almond tree.

Another unusual type is Ezequiel, who throughout the play is taken for a pathologic murderer. In truth he slays only cats for an experiment, but in recording the details of each assassination, he makes it appear as if his victims were women. Ezequiel is loved by a psychotic woman named Clotilde, whose affection for him is based on her suspicion that he dispatches his victims for purely sadistic pleasure. Yet another memorable abnormal character is the garrulous maid, Práxedes, an individual who talks to herself incessantly by asking and answering her own questions. This gallery of deranged or eccentric characters, thrown together in an excessive number of seemingly inexplicable actions and situations, is obliged to move about on a stage teeming with an outrageous number of furnishings. The play calls for the use of more physical props for a single stage setting than any other production of our time,[2] with the possible exception of Ionesco's outlandish short farce, *The New Tenant*.

As the second act draws to a close, "all of this hodgepodge," to quote Gonzalo Torrente Ballester, "regains coherence, becomes apparent, defines itself, and uncovers a tightly-bound plot, a rigorous construction, albeit labyrinthian."[3] Torrente goes on to argue, and quite correctly, that despite Jardiel's clever reintegration of all disparate elements, confusion still persists on an emotional level. While the playwright manipulates his denouement with convincing intellectual dexterity, pulling all of the loose ends together, justifying all absurdities, covering all possible angles, he leaves behind an inevitable residue of psychic bewilderment, the normal product of the play's lavish embroidery of nonsense, which clashes with the spectator's emotional need to experience a sense of verisimilitude. It is this defect which prompts Francisco Ruiz Ramón to write that Jardiel concludes such plays with "an operation of purely cerebral" exercise and always at the plot level, but never—or very few times— at the level of character development or with any concern for deeper meanings that might transcend the mere game he is playing with the construction of a complicated intrigue.[4]

Heloise contains all of the characteristics of Jardiel's passion for originality as well as all of the ingredients of that passion's intemperance. The superabundance of his audacity earned him a unique status in the annals of literary Bohemianism, yet by his singular love for the unusual and his disdain for conventionality, he incurred the wrath of a reactionary press and a tradition-bound public, became overly sensitive and defensive in the face of adverse criticism, and allowed the yahoos to canker his soul. *Heloise* marks the high point of Jardiel's long-coveted triumph in the theater, but it heralds as well the coming tempest, a climate of rancor that will ultimately lead to Jardiel's despair and will hasten his death.

II *Four Major Plays*

The following plays, together with *Heloise Lies Under an Almond Tree*, represent the quintessence of Jardielism.

A. A Round-Trip Husband (Un marido de ida y vuelta)

That Which Happened to Pepe After His Death (*Lo que le ocurrió a Pepe después de muerto*) was the awkward original title of a three-act farce produced seven months before the première of *Heloise*. Under that name it was first performed seventeen times in Barcelona, gleaning a harvest of adverse criticism, following which its title was abbreviated to *A Round-Trip Husband* for its October, 1939, première in Madrid. The play fared well in the Spanish capital and was accorded an unusual array of flattering critical reviews. In fact, the play was so well received in Madrid that some of Jardiel's most relentless adversaries tended to yield their only recorded compliments to the playwright. González Ruiz, for example, a man for whom the bulk of Jardiel's theater constitutes "a grave lack of substance . . . in which humor cedes to cruel irony or mere intranscendent comicality," singles out *A Round-Trip Husband* as the one play in which Jardiel "appears to be on the brink of success," as it possesses "a drop of intimate poetry, a light transcendental intention, and no lack of charm of situation and dialogue."[5]

The critic for whom the play was an absolute masterwork of contemporary literature was Enrique Jardiel Poncela, whose self-esteeming critique of his own work reads, in part, as follows:

A Round-Trip Husband, together with *Four Hearts in Check and Backward March, Angelina,* and *Satan's Five Warnings,* I considered in my heart to be the most perfect work of art that our imperfect human state is capable of creating. As is the case with the other three plays, it was written by subjecting the work to my personal judgment and to my own nontransferable liking, without any consideration given to others' wishes or judgments: This is the reason, perhaps, for its clamorous and wide-spread success.[6]

A Round-Trip Husband is developed along highly improbable lines. We meet the three main characters at a costume party hosted by a married couple named Leticia and Pepe. During the course of the evening Pepe extracts a promise from his best friend, Paco, that Paco will never marry Leticia in the event of Pepe's death. Then suddenly, Pepe succumbs to a heart attack. In spite of his promise, Paco does marry Leticia and this action so enrages the spirit of the departed Pepe that he returns as a ghost to reproach them both. He is still dressed in the bullfighter's costume that he had worn at the party when he died. Pepe's ghost convinces Leticia that she should leave Paco and that she should live alone until such time that she too departs mortality to join her late husband. Leticia intends to comply with Pepe's request, and does so unexpectedly: In a sudden encounter with a truck, she is run over and killed.

The reader of this brief summary will recognize at once a striking thematic parallel between Jardiel's comedy of 1939 and Noel Coward's *Blithe Spirit.* The similarities of central idea, tone, and even certain stage effects, are so marked as to suggest the possibility that the British playwright appropriated much of his material from Jardiel. In the Coward comedy, which set new performance records in London following its première at the Piccadilly Theater, July 2, 1941, it is the wife's spirit that returns to reprimand the husband and his second wife. Among the similar comic situations that can be identified in the two plays are the following: The spirit of the returning spouse is invisible for all but the former mate (Leticia/Charles Condomine); there is constant confusion produced by the crossing of dialogue because the conversation of the returning spirit (Pepe/Elvira) is inaudible to everyone but the ex-wife (Leticia) or ex-husband (Charles); the threatened party in each case (Paco/

Ruth) is victimized by the spirit's designs; great consternation is apparent by the movement of physical objects by unseen hands; and the ghost's desire to bring about a reunion with its partner brings on an accidental death.

The chief differences between the two productions lie in Coward's creation of the unforgettable comic medium, Madame Arcati, and his ironic twist at the end of *Blithe Spirit* when it is the second wife rather than the husband who dies in the accident prepared by the ghost. These departures are not sufficient, however, to justify our labeling the Coward production an entirely original work. Jardiel was not in the least amused by Noel Coward's success at the expense of his own talent and inventiveness: "My play has been greatly plagiarized abroad," he wrote.[7] And on another occasion he stated: "In my time, no writer has been more and more shamefully plagiarized than I."[8]

It is also interesting to note that Miguel Mihura and Álvaro de Laiglesia's play, *The Case of the Slightly Murdered Woman* (*El caso de la mujer asesinadita*), staged in 1946, clearly partakes of the same atmosphere as that which characterizes Jardiel's and Coward's respective works. Fernández de Asís observes that Coward's play differs considerably from Mihura's in terms of the plot line, that the correspondence is merely one of "a similar character . . . of the period."[9] Mihura's rupture with Jardiel, or Jardiel's with Mihura, was due in part to Jardiel's accusation that Mihura had plagiarized his work, a matter which Mihura continues emphatically to deny.[10]

A Round-Trip Husband has more to commend it than its historical importance as a forerunner to Noel Coward's well-known play. There are scenes, such as the opening scene of Act One, in which human foibles and pretenses are satirically depicted; and there are colorful, memorable characters, such as the servant Elías, who is imbued with a special quality that one writer has called "an undeniable mental elegance,"[11] all of which combine to make of this drama one of Jardiel's best literary writings. Marquerie declares that "everything in the work is of a prodigious hilarious force."[12] In our opinion, the two ingredients which give the play its major dynamic strength and account for its lasting reputation are, first, the high level of sophisticated humor by which the comic conflict is upheld and, second, Jardiel's tender, compassionate treatment of his characters. These are the attributes of good playwriting which, much more than those often cited as Jardiel's characteristic preoccupations—his penchant for concocting and expanding inverisimilar situations, for instance—have had the most decisive influence on the Spanish dramatists who follow Jardiel in the production of excellent humorous plays, particularly Miguel Mihura.

B. We Thieves Are Honorable People
(Los ladrones somos gente honrada)

Expanding upon the plot of a successful short story he published in *Blanco y Negro* in 1926,[13] Jardiel developed the action of *We Thieves Are Honorable People* for the express purpose of pleasing his audience:

It is not, by any means, my best play; I wouldn't even include it with that group of comedies which approach perfection [. . .]. It is purely and simply an ingenious work constructed with the highest possible technical ability. It is a play written to entertain. And from this exclusive point of view, my accomplishment could not be any greater, for in truth it did entertain, it does entertain, and it will entertain as long as Theater is Theater and the public remains the public.[14]

The play builds on a progressive swell of complications, reversals, and improbable situations, which tend to mislead and taunt the audience with a constant intermeshing of false identities, assumed names, and unsuspected surprises. It opens with the intrusion of Daniel and his band of thieves at a wealthy manor where a party to celebrate Herminia's social debut is underway. The thieves' intended assault is suddenly thwarted when Daniel falls in love with the young heroine. Although she pretends to be an older, experienced, sophisticated woman, and he tries to pass as a refined, worldly gentleman, their respective masquerades do not impede a mutual affection. Within a few months Daniel marries Herminia and brings one of his criminal companions to the mansion to serve as his butler. Two other thieves, miffed over their earlier failure to pull off the robbery, also enter the home, but they are obliged to pass as Daniel's poor relatives. This multiplication of simulation and disguise mushrooms into a hilarious game of cops and robbers. A police inspector, learning of an earlier crime involving Herminia's family, pretends to be a bungling hack detective in order to win the household's confidence. The inspector is fooled into thinking that one of the thieves, who is also attempting to clear up the mystery, is a famous sleuth. In the end, the original thieves collaborate with the police to solve the crime and receive an acquittal for their efforts. Herminia's family, on the other hand, having appeared to be honest, upright, good-natured people, are guilty of a dastardly crime. The result is a delightful farce in which the clash between appearance and reality is sustained by the exaggeration of comic situations and by an interplay of deception and subterfuge on the part of all the characters.

The playwright's clever manipulation of false clues, misleading data, and shifting suspicions enlarges the mystery to such an extent that his spectators remain as baffled as the characters appear to be. Marquerie lauds Jardiel's technical mastery over a genre he calls the most difficult challenge of stagecraft. "The interest," he writes, "does not let down even an instant. The plot is filled with constant and unexpected surprises."[15] We would add to Marquerie's words of praise that Jardiel also succeeds with this play in two interrelated ways: first, he provides us with a lively parody of a typical "whodunit" tale, allowing a preponderance of verbal tricks and stage gimmicks to function collectively as a humorous spoof on the genre. Then, at the same time, Jardiel surpasses his parodial intent to write an authentic murder mystery of his own, calculated to engage the interest of his public for an entire theater season. Indeed, the play produced for its author a total of over a quarter million pesetas in its first year on the stage and on film.[16]

C. Blanca on the Outside and Rosa Within
(Blanca por fuera y Rosa por dentro)

Conceived initially as a psychological comedy, *Blanca on the Outside and Rosa Within* proved to be an outrageous farce that sacrifices sound observation of character and solid construction for an amusing carnivalesque production employing more than the usual exaggeration of comic situations. Carried away by his fondness for shocking his audience with an incremental succession of complications derived from a single episode, Jardiel brings the action of this two-act play to a state of pandemonium. From the opening scene, whose chaos is advanced by a fierce domestic squabble between the main characters, Blanca and Ramiro, to a closing scene of cosmic disorder, with the reenactment of a train derailment in the protagonists' living room, the play can best be described as a work of sustained hilarity and madness.

The audience first views a stage setting in shambles: broken furniture, smashed dinnerware, torn draperies. Much of the exposition is provided by the servants who, after frantically trying to restore order in the wake of another epic battle between Ramiro and his temperamental wife, explain the background for the matrimonial disputes to Blanca's brother-in-law, Héctor, who is visiting the couple while en route to Patagonia. Héctor had been married to Rosa, Blanca's sister, a woman of a sterling, balanced disposition, kind, loving, generous—in all respects the opposite of Blanca. However, Rosa died in a train mishap two years previous to the play's action. Héctor, whose fondness for Blanca is quite evident, more because of her beauty than because of her shrewish character, has come to say good-bye before departing for South America. He finds himself in the middle of a quarrel of such large proportions that Ramiro and Blanca have decided to separate. Ramiro wishes to accompany Héctor to Patagonia, while his wife determines to spend an extended vacation in Andalusia. All three happen to board the same express train bound for southern Spain. A derailment occurs, similar to the one in which Rosa died. As a result of this accident, Blanca suffers a critical head injury, but survives in total amnesia and with a miraculous change in her character. She is no longer the ill-natured shrew of former times, but has taken on those gentle qualities of behavior attributed to her deceased sister. Ramiro, of course, is overjoyed. He is now married to the ideal wife: Blanca on the outside—a winsome, beautiful woman—and Rosa within, possessing all the sweetness of a genteel maid. A serious problem ensues, however, when Ramiro discovers that Blanca's new personality also includes a strong attachment for Héctor.

Since he can no longer remove the equally enamored Héctor from the scene, Ramiro determines to reconstruct the train accident in his living room as a means of restoring Blanca to her former condition. The shock treatment is a complete success. Blanca not only recovers her memory, but she returns as well to her normal state of ill-humor, bringing a fresh store of irascibility with which to torment her relieved husband.

Jardiel's inventiveness is nowhere more apparent than in this play. At one point, during the reconstructed train accident, he brings together twelve characters and engages them in simultaneous action and dialogue. He controls expertly the ironic delineation of minor comic types, such as the rattlebrained maid, Mónica, whose peculiar behavior reminds us of Práxedes' mad ways in *Heloise*, and the engaging Dr. Fonseca, who prescribes the shock treatment for Blanca's recovery. Perhaps Jardiel's most noteworthy accomplishment is achieved by the use of several distancing techniques in the Brechtian manner. In Marquerie's words, Jardiel "dehypnotizes the spectators, making them depart and then recover from the suggestion that the dialogue and the sweeping course of the action exercise upon them, obliging them to reflect and to reconsider the course of the comic or dramatic-grotesque events to which they have been a witness."[17] Even the characters seem free to identify with or to comment upon the zany proceedings. Both the real and the simulated train crashes, complete with special lighting and sound effects, signs, physical movement on and off stage, and overt parody, contribute in no small degree to establish the practical application of the so-called theory of alienation, wherein the audience observes but does not identify with the action.

D.   You and I Make Three (Tú y yo somos tres)

When *You and I Make Three* was last staged in Madrid, Adolfo Prego wrote that the play "offers a commonly acknowledged characteristic of Jardiel Poncela: the detailed and prolonged treatment of key situations evolving from a single happening."[18] That single happening concerns the marriage-by-proxy of Manolina to Rodolfo, who appears before his bride arm-in-arm with his Siamese twin, Adolfo. Manolina resolves to have the brothers separated, and thus she commissions Dr. Loriga to perform the delicate operation. Once the two men are detached, Adolfo, who exhibits certain tendencies toward being a scoundrel, departs into the world of riotous living. However, Adolfo's unrestrained dissipation effects serious consequences in Rodolfo, who suffers both physically and psychologically the results of his twin brother's extravagant behavior. Since Rodolfo cannot face the prospect of married life while still dependent in a psychic way on Adolfo, Manolina prompts an all-out effort to locate the profligate half of Rodolfo's personality. Once the prodigal is found, Dr. Loriga subjects the twins to a special therapy in order to restore to each his normal sense of individuality.

A few months following its première, the play was accorded an energetic endorsement by Alfredo Marqueríe. He devoted the last eight pages of a forty-seven-page monograph written about Jardiel's theater to *You and I Make Three*.[19] Among his several epithets of praise, Marqueríe calls the play "a revolutionary and renovating work...of exceptional comic value."[20] Impressed, perhaps, by the serious and humorous implications underlying the twins' conscious awareness that they are incapable of reaching fulfillment while reduced to a kind of infrahuman dependency, Marqueríe allows his enthusiasm for the work to color his critical judgment. Technically, it is a good play, but it is no more "revolutionary and renovating" than any single play of Jardiel's earlier successful productions. Its humor borders at times on low comedy and the situations often imply an attitude of mockery at the medical profession, reminiscent of Latin farces. The physician in this case, Dr. Loriga, is in fact a quack of quite conventional character, just another undistinguished doctor who prescribes needless treatments and who receives many satirical buffetings in the name of amusement. Aside from its capability of evoking, as Alfredo Marqueríe calculates, no less than 109 bursts of laughter in Act One and 63 in Act Two, *You and I Make Three* has little to commend it as an enduring piece of literature. With this play Jardiel has begun a long, painful, frustrating, and humiliating descent, not in terms of any loss of creativity or technical skill, but in his overinsistence on launching absurdity for its own sake and his dogged persistence in defending himself against the verbal volleys of his detractors.

III   *Plays of Secondary Importance*

During the eleven-year period which extended from the writing of *Carlo Monte* (1939) to the staging of his last play, *Tigers Hidden in the Bedroom* (1949), Jardiel Poncela's artistic plunge paralleled his physical, moral, and emotional decline. Aside from the few stellar exceptions we have recounted, namely, *A Round-Trip Husband, Heloise, Blanca on the Outside and Rosa Within*, and *You and I Make Three*, the plays which comprise the productivity of Jardiel's last decade are notably inferior to most of his previous writings. Their deficiencies reside not so much in the obvious heightening of preposterous situations (which at worst betoken a somewhat frenzied obsession to be exceptionally original, and at best consecrate Jardiel's reputation as a master of unusual inventiveness), as in the fact that his sophisticated humor often gives way to a heightened current of hysteria. Indeed, Jardiel's final productions, while technically sound, are so intensely geared to elicit a level of sustained hilarity, that they frequently overwhelm the reader or spectator by their superabundance of wit. They also convey the impression that their author is laboring to justify himself.

This profusion of fun and games with dialogue, conflict, characterization, and action has the unfortunate result of wearying the mind. There is nothing more tedious than amplified comedy. And when every expression and movement is inflated with pleasantry, without respite, amusement degenerates into embarrassment and laughter becomes an uncomfortable burden. Such is the state of vexation we experience in reading Jardiel's last long series of plays.

A.   Carlo Monte in Montecarlo (Carlo Monte en Montecarlo)

Carlo Monte is a light operetta in fourteen tableaux, another example of a work whose humor is weighed down by its own excess. The musical score is by Jacinto Guerrero. Over sixty characters comprise the cast, although Carlo Monte, the protagonist, is the focal point of the action throughout the play's many scenes. Carlo Monte is a notorious, inveterate gambler whose successes so terrify the proprietors of a Montecarlo casino that they scheme to prohibit his visit. Carlo, accompanied by Valentina, his young provincial girlfriend, surmounts all interference and boldly advances to the casino's game room. In a desperate effort to forestall his winnings, the casino's staff decides to get rid of Carlo Monte by obliging him to sign a printed letter announcing his suicide. Before the fatal event can take place, however, Carlo has the opportunity of gambling at the tables, and for the first time in his career, he loses. The proprietors are relieved and forgiving, and thus they allow Carlo and his girlfriend to depart Monaco unharmed.

The play is a lavish mockery of the financial world. Its satire is directed at the administrative personnel of the casino, at men devoted to the acquisition of wealth at any cost. In the final scenes we find some curious parallels to one of Alejandro Casona's plays of two years earlier (1937): When the casino provides pistols guaranteed not to fail and an inspector escorts the potential suicides to a nearby garden to help them choose the most romantic spot for their demise, one is reminded of Dr. Ariel's sanatorium for broken souls in Casona's charming comedy, *Suicide Is Forbidden in the Springtime* (*Prohibido suicidarse en primavera*).

B. Love Lasts Only 2000 Meters (El amor sólo dura 2000 metros)

A second illustration of a play which attempted to embrace too wide a spectrum of satire, caricature, and badinage, and as such resulted in "the most complete and solid failure of the author's theatrical career,"[21] is his stage depiction of life in Hollywood, *Love Lasts Only 2000 Meters*. This five-act comedy, which takes place in the year 1932, is replete with many of Jardiel's personal experiences in a large movie studio.[22] It concerns the misadventures and illusions of a film writer and his wife, the internationally famous actress Annie Barrett. They discover that the American movie industry is contaminated by gangsters and that personal relations between actors, directors, and producers lack all of the goodwill, kindness, and decorum they had grown to love in Europe. When his wife is victimized by corruption and his film writing goes unappreciated, the husband returns in disgust to Spain.

Everything is overstated in this bad play. The minute details of the stage setting yield a sense of oversufficiency to the production.[23] The enormous casting—nearly fifty characters—unduly crowds the action with too many busy bodies. The main roles are stereotypes, drawn with such elementary strokes as to eliminate all chances for an effective character study. Jardiel's penchant for exaggeration also vitiates the effect of good comedy: too often the humor droops and sags into superficial melodrama.

The third act of the play was greeted by a tumultuous stamping of feet which grew in force and lasted until the final curtain. *Love Last Only 2000 Meters* was an artistic failure, the critics decried its worst faults, the public manifested no support or sympathy for the play, and Jardiel became greatly embittered over the whole sad experience.

C. Mother, The Father Drama (Madre, el drama padre)

Jardiel's failure with *Love Lasts Only 2000 Meters* was followed by a confused and confusing phantasmagoria of quasi-surrealistic satire that he entitled *Mother, The Father Drama*. A caricature of modern melodramas, set in Madrid, the action of this play piles up multiple complications that twist and spiral toward delirium. It concerns the marriage of four twin girls to four twin boys. Following the ceremony, an uncle appears and declares that all eight of the young people are truly brothers and sisters and that, consequently, their marriage is null and void. The ensuing action revolves about the many inquiries into the origin of this disconcerting claim. The investigation discloses several possibilities of illegitimacy, adultery, incest, and multiple deceptions. Finally it is learned that there is no truth to the uncle's charge. But when the happy tidings are about to be conveyed to the eight principals, their families and friends discover that all four couples have eloped, determined to preserve their happiness at any cost.

Jardiel's use of irony is manifest as he pans the silliness of tragicomic melodramas based on vulgar tales of extramarital problems, illegitimate births, and confused parental ties. However, this misunderstood intention invited a backlash of criticism from Madrid's conservative critics, who labeled the work "absolutely immoral" and then initiated a declaration of official censorship against the play.[24] When the smoke cleared, *Mother, The Father Drama* was reinstated and enjoyed over one hundred sixty performances, its popularity due mainly to the fact that its adverse publicity in the Spanish press attracted many new curious patrons.

D.   It's Dangerous to Look Outside
       (Es peligroso asomarse al exterior)

Two other aggressive satires followed *Mother, The Father Drama*. Both were fashioned as an attack on "the inanity, the insipidity, and the affectation" of popular movies and plays of the early 1940's.[25] In the first, entitled *It's Dangerous to Look Outside*, three men are engaged to the same woman. Isabel met each of them in successive encounters in Buenos Aires, New York, and Nice. She has been able to assume the personality that fits each one of her suitors and thereby forgets about her other attachments. Moreover, each of the men molds his being into the kind of personality that Isabel expects of him. This process of self-duplicity enables each person to discover his own weaknesses and to confess them openly. Further complications ensue over questions of love and deception involving the other girlfriends of each suitor. Isabel finally manages to resolve the multiple dilemmas by assisting to pair off the various couples to everyone's satisfaction.

Jardiel's purpose in writing this mediocre farce was to aim a comic criticism at the many works of psychological love adventures in vogue at the time. The play's humor and meaning are derived from two levels, namely, the surface level of action in which constant misunderstandings complicate the lives of all the characters, and the psychological level which underlies the play's thesis, that no one person is any more nor less authentic than how other people perceive him.[26] The rapid movement and expanding complexity of the action, together with Jardiel's fond use of irony as each character reveals his moral defects, account for the play's commercial success of 231 performances.

E.   The Inhabitants of the Uninhabited House
   (Los habitantes de la casa deshabitada)

The companion satire to *It's Dangerous to Look Outside* was also premièred in 1942 with another title of typical Jardielesque contradiction: *The Inhabitants of the Uninhabited House.* The plot of this two-act comedy centers around a loud and stimulating ghost story. It concerns the retreat by two men, a journalist and his chauffeur, to an abandoned country home in the province of Salamanca. In the darkness they hear strange piano music and a woman's screams. Frightened but too curious to leave, the men attempt to uncover the mystery. The journalist discovers one of his former sweethearts hiding out in the house. She admits to being terrified by floating objects, a headless man, and a walking skeleton. In the course of their investigation, they learn that the ghosts are merely sophisticated props manipulated by a gang of counterfeiters. The criminals have endeavored to frighten away intruders who might otherwise detect their presence.

The author's professed aim in writing this unusual work of fantasy is to point to the absurdity of many untheatrical productions of his time, that is, the "common, believable comedies of small conflict, foolish intrigue, and stupid problems" to which the public turned with applause, rejoicing, and emotion.[27] Jardiel defends the free flow of the imagination and proposes to fill his stage with the most unconventional devices known to stagecraft. He rejects every commonplace prop by relying on highly theatrical gimmicks to help expound his message. Insisting, further, that a good play should captivate and hold the audience's interest without recourse to inane domestic prattle or insipid intrigues, he substitutes strange happenings (appearance of phantoms, moving furniture) and audible or visual surprises (weird noises, eerie lights) for the more common moments of normal repartee. *The Inhabitants of the Uninhabited House* is a work that maximizes the use of unusual paraphernalia to minimize the conventions of sound characterization and unified action. Abnormalities abound over good sense.

We are uncertain as to what extent Jardiel's understanding or misunderstanding of alienation as a stage technique may have influenced his preference for special objects and props. The audience is granted a reduced opportunity to identify subjectively with the characters or events. One distancing element becomes apparent in the journalist's assuming the role of spectator; he often withdraws from the immediate concerns of the haunted house to become a cold, objective viewer of the action. Jardiel's stage tricks, the racket and frenzy on stage, the flashing of lights, the mysterious movement of furnishings destroy further any illusion of reality. In Brecht this apparent chaos would convey the substance of an important social message, but with Jardiel there is no enduring lesson conveyed to the spectator. This notwithstanding Jardiel's professed satiric intent as recorded in the play's prologue. But this surface amusement sufficed to assure Jardiel an unprecedented commercial success: The play set a record of over 450 performances during its first run in Madrid.

F.   The Cat's Seven Lives (Las siete vidas del gato)

Mystery as the primary thrust also forms the basis of Jardiel's next play, a two-act melodrama of intrigue entitled *The Cat's Seven Lives*. As was the case with *Angelina*, the action begins late in the nineteenth century and then, as in the development of *Four Hearts in Check and Backward March*, it unfolds in progressive stages until we arrive at the present. With successive glimpses into the past, we learn that Guillermo's family history is shrouded in an evil curse. Six women have been assassinated by men in the family. According to the tradition, still another female must die. Guillermo, recently married and now filled with terror over the thought that he will be his wife's slayer, flees from her side and goes into hiding. His bride, however, is charmed over the notion that her husband might indeed take her life; compelled by a romantic death wish, she goes to seek him out. Together they await her tragic destiny at his hands. When a black cat appears, the sign given immediately before each previous murder, she knows that her time has come. Suddenly Guillermo's cousin, Luz María, who secretly loves him and who

is running from the clutches of her angry guardian, appears.
During a conversation between Luz María and Guillermo's wife
a shot rings out. Luz María drops to the floor, victim of her
guardian's wrath. And thus the family's sinister prophesy is
fulfilled.

Jardiel's control with intrigue and suspense is remarkably
keen. Following the course he pursued in *The Inhabitants of the
Uninhabited House*, he brings together multiple dramatic, tragic,
and grotesque elements, woven within the framework of banter
and showmanship.[28] His overall satiric aim is directed at the
foolishness of superstition. One interesting feature is that, quite
unlike the rest of Jardiel's theater, wherein playful cynicism
pervades the action, in *The Cat's Seven Lives* he assumes a
hopeful, positive posture concerning the value and joy of living.
Marquería designates this atypical cheerfulness as "the pure
and poetic exaltation of courage and optimism."[29] In this regard,
the play suggests certain parallels of tone and attitude with the
idealistic theater of Casona.

G. The Wandering Lady's Handkerchief
    (El pañuelo de la dama errante)

In his tragicomedy in two acts, *The Wandering Lady's Handkerchief*, Jardiel again develops a plot based on suspense and
intrigue and uses strange objects to enhance his atmosphere of
fantasy. Unlike the funfare of his previous ghost play, this
enigmatic work borders on the time-honored literary motif of
illusion versus reality. Dreams, symbolism, and unusual images
seem to have a meaning that would transcend the simple caprice
of comic inventiveness. Somewhere in his maze of free imaginative subplots lies an important message. But where? And
what is it?

The action occurs in an old shabby palace filled with mysterious secrets, prisoners in armor, and sundry delirious persons,
including the floating ghost of the Wandering Lady. Into this
sanctum comes Lolita, a poor girl who has been duped into believing that she is heiress to an enormous fortune. The phantom
of a murdered countess appears to Lolita, leaving as proof of
her ethereal existence a pretty lace handkerchief. In the course

of the ensuing action, Lolita's prize legacy is stolen several times by the palace's demented inhabitants, but the friendly ghost always manages to retrieve it. Ultimately, the hoax that was perpetrated on Lolita is upended and with the aid of her spectral friend, Lolita becomes the true heiress. Having served her function as a disembodied playmate to Lolita in their ghostly game of "finders-keepers" with a supernatural handkerchief, the female spook disappears, failing to reveal her full identity or the true meaning of this creepy, rather silly play.

Even Alfredo Marqueríe, Jardiel's indefatigable champion and explicator, is hard pressed to interpret the meaning of *The Wandering Lady's Handkerchief*. He is content to explain away its prevailing enigmas as being the result of Jardiel's deliberate effort "to open windows to the impossible and to vivify the scene with the gentle breeze of imagination, wherein reality is not clear and simple, close to earth, but is an invention filled with illusion."[30] Substantive defects still remain to haunt us, nevertheless. The protagonist's role is central to this problem: Is Lolita a mad, hysterical woman who sees the elusive spirit only in her imagination? Or is she the innocent victim of an outlandish practical joke? Who are her real friends? Those who enable her to become the heiress by their participation in the charade? Or those who attempt to save her from a cruel hoax? Jardiel's dalliance with the real and the fictitious produces a fine defense in favor of his free use of imagination, but it also leaves us with a work crying out for deliverance from ambiguity and irresolution.

H. Water, Oil and Gasoline (Agua, aceite y gasolina)

The première of *Water, Oil and Gasoline* was an unfortunate disaster. A group of dissenters, predisposed to greet the new comedy with a barrage of footstomping, hoots, hollers, and hissings, began a demonstration six minutes into the first act and continued in crescendo until the final curtain. The rude reception has been registered as "the most tremendous and violent uproar in the history of the Spanish theater."[31] It gave rise to two public overreactions, the one a souring on the part of the news media towards Jardiel's talents, the other a tirade of defensive warfare authored by Jardiel against his critics.[32] From this time on, Jardiel relished but few moments of satisfaction during any première performance; of his remaining three plays, two were strongly berated by spectators and assailed by the critics, and one, an exceptionally good work, was ignored.

Water, Oil and Gasoline deals with the amorous involvement of Mario, a famous writer, with a married woman. When his mistress decides not to forsake her husband and to stop seeing Mario, the protagonist suffers a near collapse of emotional anguish. In order to cure him from his state of depression, his physician finds a young girl from the lower class whom he trains and dresses to impersonate the former mistress and thus disabuse Mario of his illusions. The girl flounders hopelessly in her assumed role, but her blunders have the surprising effect of impressing Mario that she is a remarkably fine woman. When the former mistress returns, having decided to rekindle Mario's affection for her, he fails to recognize any physical difference between her and her impersonator, but he remarks that he dislikes the way she has changed and hopes she will continue to conduct herself as she had lately been accustomed. The real mistress departs in anger, leaving Mario free to marry his now authentic lover.

The unjust abuse accorded this work has tended to relegate its title to near oblivion. The dramatist's chief apologists—Alfredo Marquerie and Rafael Flórez—fail to mention the play in the text of their respective books, essays, and articles. The play has not even been granted the dubious privilege of a listing among Jardiel's worst plays. One might suspect that its tumultuous première divested the writing of its very existence in the history of the modern Spanish theater. There is adequate justification, however, for vindicating this four-act comedy, if for no other reason than the fact that the characterization of Cosqui, the illiterate, low-class waif whose rustic speech, drab appearance, and uncouth conduct are gradually refined into the exquisite mannerisms of an elegant lady, is an accomplishment of superb comic force, a model worthy of comparison with Shaw's Eliza Doolittle.

I. The Weaker Sex Has Undergone Gymnastics
(El sexo débil ha hecho gimnasia)

While *Water, Oil and Gasoline* made its short, sad run at
Madrid's Zarzuela Theater, Jardiel was writing one of his finest
but most underrated comedies, *The Weaker Sex Has Undergone
Gymnastics*. He spent considerable time completing this play,
owing to the fact that he was entering the early stage of the
painful, mortifying disease which was to drain his physical and
emotional strength during the ensuing months and years. His
daughter Evangelina informs us that Jardiel's acute suffering was
exacerbated by the painful realization that, following the play's
successful première, the Madrid press made no mention of the
comedy's having been conferred the coveted Jacinto Benavente
Award as the best play of the 1946 theater season.[33]

The Weaker Sex contrasts sequentially two eras of feminist
sentiment. The first part, conceived with a serious tone and
written in verse, takes place in 1846. The second, charged with
comedy and written in prose, takes place a hundred years later.
In the nineteenth-century episode, Jardiel presents a group of
six sisters of assorted ages who live with their Aunt Adelaida.
Each member of this female entourage suffers her own respective
tragedy. One girl receives a letter from her suitor informing her
that he is married already and she cannot run off with him. Another is the sweetheart of a frustrated poet who is so shattered
by failure when his first play is laughed at that he commits
suicide. A third sister, finding she is pregnant and deserted by
her lover, gives up the baby to a charitable organization and
enters a convent. Still another, hopeful that her timid boyfriend
will propose marriage, waits too long and loses him altogether.
The one married sister is forced to abandon her singing talent as
well as her family because of her husband's tyrannical conduct.
Even the baby sister, who speaks with a strong lisp, has her own
personal calamity: her little female dog dies for lack of adequate
exercise. Adelaida, their strong-willed aunt, is the final victim
of this downtrodden feminist fate. She is obliged to turn down
her last hope of marriage in order to continue caring for her
unfortunate nieces. Adelaida is the spokesman for the sad plight
of woman in a man's world, and she laments the fact that

women are the victims of injustice, oppression, and male chauvinist attitudes. Someday, she declares, the weaker sex will take up gymnastics and become strong.

In Part Two, the changes that a hundred years have wrought show up in vivid contrast with the milieu of the unhappy nineteenth century. New characters, with new names and new dispositions, take the place of the former roles, although the same actresses play the parts. The situations are now all reversed: each woman controls her own destiny. Each is confronted by the same calamity as her ninetennth-century counterpart, but no one succumbs to failure. The girl whose fiancé admits to being married takes the news calmly and then sues him for breach of promise. The one whose poet-boyfriend was crushed over failure takes over the management of his literary career and spurs him on to success. The unwed pregnant sister whose suitor abandoned her is overjoyed with the prospect of raising her child without the burden of an unwanted husband. The girl with the shy boyfriend proposes marriage to him rather than let him get away. And the talented married sister who in 1846 gave up her career because of her despotic mate, is now a famous singer and her husband docilely follows her around, caring for her luggage. Even the kid sister is a high-spirited, emancipated woman. She no longer lisps, but eavesdrops, blackmails, sells confidential information, and, in general, behaves like a liberated brat. Furthermore, her dog gets so much exercise that it has one litter after another. And Aunt Adelaida herself, who is now Aunt Lila—the women all have rare and exotic names to go with their new freedom—offers a liberal, optimistic outlook on life. As we might expect, she now marries her admirer rather than sacrifice personal happiness for her 1846 role of servitude.

Aside from Jardiel's predisposition to accumulate exaggerations for comic effect, a practice we observe particularly in the second part wherein the sisters' antics often approach absurdity, this extremely funny modern work is structured with an expert manipulation of control, vivacity, and daring equal to that of Jardiel's more youthful writings. Each situation in Part Two is doubly amusing because of its contrast with the tragic developments of Part One. Jardiel's view of the past, contrived poetically to satirize a period in which verse drama was the frequent vehicle of expression in the theater, shows no nostalgic attachment for "the good old days." At best, his revival of former memories, far from prompting sentimental thoughts, is calculated to create an atmosphere of caricature, much along the same line of his earlier parody on nineteenth-century melodrama, *Angelina.* The playwright's clear preference for the contemporary period allows that caricature to convey a marked distinction between the somber, harsh life for womankind of one hundred years ago and the new emergence of social and individual emancipation today.

J.   Blondes Go Better with Potatoes
     (Como mejor están las rubias es con patatas)

Incongruity swells to the most audacious proportions with Jardiel's penultimate comedy. Its title alone would suffice to confer upon this play the kind of notoriety it earned in an unkind way the night of its première: the distinction of manifesting a total abandon to theatrical abnormalities. Jardiel was deeply hurt by the public's disparagement of *Blondes Go Better with Potatoes.* Rafael Flórez speaks of "the contagious collective hysteria" which swept Madrid's theatergoing public in its denunciation of the two-act *humorada,*[34] a phenomenon that contributed in no small way to increase the ailing playwright's grief.

The play calls for a large cast of twenty-seven characters. Its zany plot concerns the disappearance and subsequent reappearance of Dr. Ulises Marabú, a noted professor of paleontology, while on an expedition in Africa. News reaches his home that the professor has become an anthropophagite as a consequence of his having lived among a tribe of cannibals. His family is especially distressed because the professor's wife, who assumed he had long ago perished, is now remarried. Marabú is returned to civilization locked in a cage in order to preclude his eating any of his former friends. In the end, the general consternation is somewhat alleviated when it is learned that the cannibal in question is really the husband of the concierge and not Ulises Marabú. Many accessory complications entangle this central issue. One is the immobilized state of three characters who are so shocked to learn that Marabú is returning home in a cage that they sit frozen to a sofa throughout most of the play. The concierge and her daughter sell admission tickets and conduct guided tours to the room where the strange creatures are seated, and this action leads to a further multiplication of human statues. Other involvements include the appearance of radio announcers with members of the family, assorted strangers, a man who thinks he is a bird, and a caged cannibal who is busy writing a cookbook. To confuse the atmosphere more, Jardiel presents a number of characters consistently speaking in an incomprehensible jumble of foreign languages. All in all, explicit caricature and satire are cheapened by a collateral dash of sheer madness in action and in dialogue, reminiscent at times of Ionesco, but more akin to the frivolous trappings of a circus revue than to the acknowledged function and purpose of the theater of the absurd.

Clearly, this play is a highly sophisticated put-down of pedantry. One of the absent-minded professors in the cast is so completely unaware of what is happening around him that he loses all contact with reality. Whenever someone manages to distract him from his thoughts, he answers by saying that class is over and the students may leave. When Marabú disappears in Africa, he receives great recognition at home: A street bears his name, a statue is erected in his honor. But when the news reaches Spain that Marabú has been found and will be returning home, one of the characters asks if the statue will be torn down and the street renamed now that Marabú is alive and well. Unfortunately, though, many of the searching questions Jardiel suggests concerning the nature of an important man's reputation in and contributions to society are dimmed by the spectacle of ludicrous, bizarre, and foolish happenings.

K. Tigers Hidden in the Bedroom
       (Los tigres escondidos en la alcoba)

Only those of us who were close to him know at what cost he was able to write this play. His illness consumed him by slow degrees, and writing was an exhausting experience for him. He had a will of iron and he worked a great deal, all that he could; but he didn't regain the strength that he rendered in writing.[35]

This is the testimony of Evangelina Jardiel Poncela about her father's final work, *Tigers Hidden in the Bedroom*, a two-act comedy of intrigue premièred in January of 1949. The excessive length and variegated intricacies of the play prompted some critics to label it an interminable play, but aside from Jardiel's generosity with his script, there was little for them to criticize adversely about his last effort.[36]

The "tigers" of the title are a band of international jewel thieves who victimize the guests of luxury hotels. They move into an expensive suite, carefully prepare it for a future robbery, then move out. The new tenants, however, uncover all the electronic devices for facilitating the crime and then manage to substitute an identical jewel case for the real one. From this moment on, the plot thickens with customary Jardielesque artifice. This includes the introduction of an unsolved murder mystery from several years before; a rivalry between the head bandit and the man who poses as his valet; a misunderstanding between the maid, who is a thief in disguise, and the manicurist, who is really a secret agent for a policeman currently posing as a blackmailer; the appearance of a demented female; and a woman who claims to be her brother-in-law's wife. The comic chaos which results from this highly complicated plot requires a successful recollection of all previous details to bring about some semblance of rationality when the play is done. Yet it is all complete; the entanglements are unwoven and rewoven quite nicely into place. To the spectator who has followed the acceleration of the comic action, with its sudden reversals, exciting contrasts, and distorted logic, belongs a special sense of relief when the entire ludicrous enterprise has extracted its last reaction from the audience. Jardiel's illness aside, it is no wonder he was so completely exhausted upon concluding the last of his well-nigh incredible plays, a work of excessive incongruity.

IV *Minor Writings: Monologues and One-Act Plays*

Few authors openly repudiate more than half their finished products. Jardiel Poncela must have established some kind of record with his emphatic rejection of over fifty completed plays, spanning a twelve-year period. Approximately one-half of his disowned comedies were written in collaboration with Serafín Adame Martínez, part of the prolific productivity of his apprenticeship years to which we referred earlier. Close to one-third of those plays would fall under the classification of *entremeses* or *pasos*, that is, one-act farces specifically designed to entertain and amuse the audience and often intended as comic accompaniments to more lengthy productions. Despite his eagerness to disown his repertory of those many compressed writings he labeled as mediocre experiments, Jardiel never lost his fondness for cultivating the short skit. He found in such minor dramatic modes a suitable form for making succinct satiric comments on the absurdity of the human condition. Frequently he reduced his script to a simple monologue for the delivery of a comic routine not unlike that expounded on popular television by contemporary comedians. Among these short routines was a series of delightful monologues written for several important actresses: Catalina Bárcena, Isabel Garcés, and María Paz Molinero.

Two of Jardiel's edited playlets merit special mention. The first, a one-act *entremés* consisting of only four characters, was premièred the same year as *Blanca on the Outside and Rosa Within* and *The Cat's Seven Lives* (1943). This charming little farce, entitled *At Six O'Clock on the Corner of the Boulevard* (*A las seis, en la esquina del bulevár*), elaborates a simple situation in a relatively simple manner. Two women disagree over the marital devotion of Rodrigo. Cecilia, his wife, maintains that Rodrigo is completely faithful and could withstand any challenge. Casilda, his former mistress, cynically believes that Rodrigo will succumb to temptation if put to the test. The women agree to send Rodrigo, by way of the doorman, an anonymous letter in which they invite him, under the assumed name of an unknown woman, to a rendezvous at a certain corner at six o'clock that day. Cecilia and Casilda observe the corner from the window of a friend's house for three hours, but Rodrigo never appears. Cecilia is overjoyed, boasting of her victory and of her husband's fidelity. But at that moment Rodrigo returns home in a rage, because, as he explains, the doorman had only just given him a letter that summoned him for an important business appointment, and he was already three hours late.

Casilda smirks triumphantly as the disillusioned wife realizes that her husband is a cad.

The playlet's simplicity represents a moment of serenity and respite from the untoward exaggerations and the fantastic complications of the several plays which immediately precede and follow it. Characteristically, however, Jardiel's cynical outlook is fully present. With one deft sardonic stroke, he defines the unceremonious ritual of the double standard, while probing mischievously into the world of the female psyche in its helpless response to the male-dominated society of his time.

Occasionally a playwright will prepare a one-act sketch to celebrate a particular moment in his dramatic career. Jardiel responded to this option to commemorate the one hundredth performance of *You and I Make Three* on December 5, 1945, in Madrid's Teatro de la Comedia, by writing one of his most successful short pieces, a comic *paso* entitled *The Love of the Cat and the Dog* (*El amor del gato y del perro*). The casting for this brief dialogue calls for only two characters, one a young girl, the other a middle-aged man. The girl, seeking a formula for life's happiness, makes an appointment to interview a writer to ask his advice about the meaning of love. As he begins his dissertation, she listens with avid curiosity, but then, as his theories take root in her heart and she adds her own thoughts on the subject, the two discover that they were meant for one another. The *paso* contains many typical Jardielesque lines of a fast and clever repartee. It is an ideal modern interlude for staging during the entr'acte of a longer and perhaps more serious production.

CHAPTER 4

The Novels

AS was the case with his published theater writings, which were preceded by a large volume of unpublished comedies, Jardiel Poncela produced a considerable body of prose fiction long before he published his first of four major novels in 1929.[1] From the age of eighteen to the year 1929, when Jardiel turned twenty-eight, he wrote close to thirty short novels, publishing most of them in assorted literary magazines.[2] Between 1929 and 1932 he entered the arena of lengthy humoristic novels then dominated by such names as Juan Pérez Zúñiga, Joaquín Belda, Julio Camba, and Wenceslao Fernández Flórez. The four titles he contributed to the genre of comic fiction brought widespread attention to his name and established his reputation in the minds of some critics as a promising novelist whose incisive comic inventiveness would mature to such proportions as to over-shadow his labor in the theater.

I Love Is Written Without the Letter 'H'
(Amor se escribe sin hache)

Don Ramón Gómez de la Serna, regarded as the Picasso of Spanish literature because of his fecund talent and bizarre eccentricity, a man whose literary manner has generated perhaps the greatest influence on twentieth-century Spanish letters, de-termined the course of Jardiel's novelistic career early in 1928 by introducing his young friend to José Ruiz-Castillo, then founder and director of one of Madrid's oldest and most presti-gious publishing firms, Biblioteca Nueva. Ruiz-Castillo promptly invited Jardiel to submit to him a lengthy manuscript for the publisher's newly established series of humorous novels. On

October 10, 1928, Jardiel signed a contract to that effect, and within six months he had completed his first major work of prose fiction, a work of nearly 150,000 words carrying the unusual title, *Love Is Written Without the Letter 'H'*

This novel, a parody on the typical illicit intrigue to be found in subliterary works of erotic fiction, is divided into three books. The first is designated "Terceto," in reference to the husband, the wife, and the lover. It serves to introduce us to the three main characters whose incongruous triangular arrangement satirizes the amorous adventure tales which infested the numerous serials and cheap novels of Jardiel's time.

Lady Sylvia Brums, an English aristocrat whose elegant breeding includes an abundance of refined sinning, endures a humdrum existence of free love until she meets Paco Arencibia, a stupid young skeptic of high society. Following her marriage to Paco, Lady Sylvia's boredom increases. She flits from one man to another, hoping to diminish the tedium produced by marriage and too many extramarital entanglements. Her husband adds his own dash of cynicism to her adventures by writing letters to each of his wife's lovers, congratulating them on their conquest and conferring upon them the right to make love to Lady Sylvia. At last Lady Sylvia encounters the exciting, exceptional lover of her dreams, an idealistic and outspoken financier named Zambombo, who is so offended by the congratulatory missive from her husband that he provokes a duel with Paco. Neither man is injured, but Paco decides to allow Zambombo the privilege of living with his wife, well assured that in the course of time the young gallant's eyes will be opened to reality. The first book ends with the flight of Lady Sylvia and her lover to Paris.

Book Two is entitled "Dúo," typifying the wife and the lover. The satirical thrust of this section is aimed at the romance of travel and the thrill of an international liaison. On their way to Paris, Lady Sylvia and Zambombo meet various fast-living adventurers, among them Mignonne, a French lass who represents the seductive charm of loose virtue. Zambombo, with his provincial candor, finds himself ill-suited to keep pace with the elegant suitors who pay their respects to Lady Sylvia. And Lady Sylvia herself is fast becoming bored with Zambombo. In his desperation to recapture her waning love, he engages in a series of zany, absurd acts, such as disguising himself as a phantom to pretend a nocturnal assault. Finally the two lovers abandon Paris for Amsterdam, then on to London. In each city they visit, the notion is repeated that one can love equally well in Madrid as in every other cosmopolitan center. Their grand tour of the continent in search for joyous fulfillment eventually leads to a shipwreck at sea and their escape from the sea to a deserted island. However, unlike the exotic and sensual episode one might anticipate at this juncture in the typical novel of erotic adventure, Jardiel has his heroine, who is by now hopelessly bored, leave Zambombo after a short, miserable stay on the island.

The final book is entitled "Romanza," or "The Lover." Jardiel's focus now comes to bear on the complete physical and moral deterioration of his protagonist, Zambombo, who, having returned to Madrid, is now a bitter and forlorn man. In contrast to his bearing in Book One, he is shorn of all idealism. Seeking moral support for his pessimistic view of the world, he drops in on Paco Arencibia, Lady Sylvia's deserted husband. But to his astonishment, Zambombo finds that Paco is incommunicable, having fallen madly in love with the French prostitute Mignonne, whom he has mistaken for a sweet schoolgirl. In the final chapters, Zambombo, now a complete cynic, renews his acquaintance with Fermín, a boyhood friend. As a result of a ludicrous adventure they have together, Zambombo inherits a great fortune, and thus the narrative ends. The hero's faith in the goodness of life is restored, thanks to his fortuitous attainment of wealth.

In the last chapter, the meaning behind the novel's title is made clear. Fermín and Zambombo engage in a curious dialogue recounting the excellence behind words which begin with the letter *h*. Among the many examples of important h-words cited, it is observed that the word *amor* is noticeably absent; love must therefore be relegated to a level of relative insignificance.

How effective is Jardiel's parody on the exaggerations of popular love novels? His detractors were quick to accuse the author of an overzealous aspiration to rival the accomplishment of Cervantes, who apparently aimed at putting an end to the widespread proliferation of mediocre tales of chivalry by writing the greatest adventure novel of all time. Yet Jardiel's

expressed intent to undo a vogue of erotic literature with one
irreverent pastiche—a fact he makes apparent in the preface to
this first novel[3]—cannot be taken seriously. He may have had in
mind what he took as the *Quijote's* literary mission, but the
cynical good humor of his writing conveys at best a spirit of
burlesque that falls short of acceptable literary substance. The
novel's content suggests, in fact, the possibility that Jardiel may
have promoted a greater rash of erotic literature in Spain than
to have purged the genre of its virulence.[4] Had he intended
this novel to be more than a cynical chortle, there is no evidence
beyond his use of zany episodes, accumulated for mere comic
effect, to vindicate the effort. We lean strongly to the belief that
Jardiel's avowed proposal to sweep away a prevailing current
of contemptible literature was but an affirmation of farce, a
simple comic gesture, in that he seized upon a popular subliterary current by which to develop and circulate his own
spicy banter.[5]

The parody does demonstrate, however, that Jardiel is an
assiduous reader of the European novel of erotic adventure. His
reaction in burlesque to the epidemic of sexual topics provides
an interesting survey of the stereotyped devices employed by
French and Spanish writers of the period. Using humor to de-
base the commonplace themes of a literature he calls "alkaloid"
in substance, Jardiel repeats and satirizes many of the empty
clichés found in the erotic novels of Jean Lorrain and Mme
Alfred Valette ("Rachilde") of France[6] and Alberto Insúa,
Rafael López de Haro, Felipe Trigo, Antonio de Hoyos y
Vinent, and Eduardo Zamacois of Spain.[7] The amorous misdeeds of audacious men and wanton ladies constituted the
literary offerings of the aforenamed novelists. One critic singled
out fifty-two names of Spanish authors whose mediocre publications capitalized to such an extent on the public's demand for
sensuous topics that by the first quarter of the twentieth cen-
ury erotic writings predominated over all other forms of literature.[8] A few isolated protests were voiced by members of the
literary intelligentsia of Spain, such as Pío Baroja, who wrote
an essay on the subject,[9] and the literary historian Julio Cejador
y Frauca, who vehemently condemned this tendency as "cerebral voluptuosity and morbid eroticism...of insufferable

Parisian literature."[10] The hue and cry did little to diminish the mushrooming of naughty novelettes. Jardiel, believing that adverse criticism would only fan the public's interest in the plague, chose rather to deride the grandiloquent style, the commonplace phraseology, and the exotic unrealistic themes in vogue through the use of humorous parody. His position is made implicit by irony and rendered explicit by frequent asides to the reader: he ridicules the entire legacy of prostituted love, international philandering, and cosmopolitan escapades bequeathed to novelists of his generation by such celebrated writers as the Italian Gabriele d'Annunzio and the German authoress Vicki Braum.

One favorable aspect of Jardiel's first novel resides in the author's ability to campaign against the lurid prescriptions of amorous tales without reducing his three protagonists to absolute caricature. Neither the wife (Lady Sylvia), the husband (Paco Arencibia), nor the lover (Zambombo) loses his identity as a winsome and sympathetically-drawn character. In general they represent the satiety of love, the frustrating difficulty of maintaining social appearances, and what one critic calls "the masquerade of sentimental and sensual frustration."[11] But like any believable characters of prose fiction, they ponder, plot, and weep within the framework of their respective personalities; their development is consistent with the action. Above all, they engage in the kind of delectable intellectual repartee one usually associates with the characters of Oscar Wilde or Bernard Shaw, and thus they oblige the reader to equate the candid cynicism they express as fictional beings of a cosmopolitan society with their creator's skeptical view of the world. In this connection Lacosta is not far wrong in viewing Zambombo as the personification of Jardiel Poncela,[12] for it is by way of Zambombo's verbal ingenuousness and deft raillery that the author conveys to us his most caustic depreciation of escapist literature. In *Love Is Written Without the Letter 'H'*, the hero is at once a flesh-and-blood character and a purveyor of Jardiel's message, a laughable and nimble-witted buffoon and intelligent spokesman who lampoons the tedious and trite conventions of dime novel romances.

II   Wait for Me in Siberia, My Love
(Espérame en Siberia, vida mía)

Jardiel Poncela was not yet twenty-eight when he wrote his second successful novel, during a three and one-half month period in 1926. According to Canay, for whom everything Jardiel accomplished was of transcendental importance, the "clamorous success" of *Love Is Written Without the Letter 'H'* could only be followed by the "thunderous success" of *Wait for Me in Siberia, My Love*.[13] We venture to temper the extravagance of Canay's adjectives by suggesting that both novels did indeed enjoy favorable public acclaim, but that no new sales records were broken by their respective publications.

Siberia is a comic miscellany of adventure travels. The hero's name, Mario Esfarcies, like that of the lover in Jardiel's previous novel, is as incongruous as are his journeyings over the European continent. Mario Esfarcies is a stylish young man of considerable wealth who is loved by the beautiful, sinful Palmera Suaretti, a woman of high ambition and low scruples. She in turn is not loved by Mario, but endures instead the weepy advances of a fifty-year-old Marquis who adores and adorns her body. Mario, of course, loves another, to whom he is betrothed. On the final night of his bachelorhood, he becomes so hopelessly inebriated that Palmera attempts to exploit his condition to her own advantage. Failing however to seduce him, she takes him to his home, believing that she has lost him forever.

Esfarcies awakens the following day, only to collapse with a severe stomach ailment, the result of his intoxication. Fearing a serious malady, he hastens to visit his old friend, Dr. Joaquín Faber, whom Jardiel portrays as an unscrupulous and incompetent practitioner. Faber is as penniless as he is unprincipled, and knowing that his wealthy friend Mario is gullible and trusting, the evil doctor plots to acquire his fortune. Faber diagnoses terminal cancer of the stomach and persuades the despairing Mario to name him heir of his entire estate. Esfarcies agrees and promptly determines to kill himself. After a series of fruitless efforts to end his own life, he contracts the service of a professional killer. According to their agreement, the hired assassin, named Poresosmundos, will eliminate Mario by surprise. But unknown to Mario, the wicked Dr. Faber, eager to inherit the doomed man's money, has offered the assassin double his fee to expedite the execution.

To his relief and grief, Esfarcies discovers the doctor's treachery. While he now knows he will not die in agony with cancer, it is too late to retract the contract on his life, for Poresosmundos is lurking somewhere not too far away, determined to murder him. Having broken off his engagement with his girlfriend, Mario now runs to the arms of Palmera Suaretti, begging for her assistance to protect him from the hired assassin. He finally decides to flee to far-off Siberia and asks Palmera to meet him there.

Jardiel devotes a large portion of the novel to Mario's travels about Europe, pursued by the unrelenting killer. Over seas and across many lands, the two men journey, the hero escaping miraculously one attempt on his life after another. Finally the assassin and Mario, tired of running and pursuing, make a pact of friendship, and Esfarcies returns happily to Madrid, free of anguish and fear, no longer compelled to hide in Siberia, and disposed to make love to Palmera in her own apartment.

Then it happens. After countless attempts to commit suicide and after seven thousand kilometers of flight from certain death at the hands of a professional killer, Mario suddenly trips while ascending the staircase toward Palmera's apartment, and falls backwards to his death. The lovely Palmera Suaretti, saddened momentarily by her prospective lover's inopportune demise, seeks comfort in the presence of the kind old Marquis, the same one who had solicited her attentions from the beginning. The novel ends with Palmera becoming the Marquis' mistress. And no one seems to remember the late Mario Esfarcies.

In many ways, *Siberia* is cast in the same mold as Jardiel's first novel. The chase across Europe, with Poresosmundos in pursuit of Mario Esfarcies, resembles the cosmopolitan pilgrimage of Zambombo and Sylvia in *Love Is Written Without the Letter 'H'*. The absurd love entanglements depicted satirically in the early chapters of *Siberia* have the same spirit of parody which flavors the episodic dalliances of the first novel. The characters are again employed to ridicule the exotic aura of adulterous love, adventuresome travel, and social pretense which is spewed forth plentifully in the prevailing literature that precedes the outbreak of the Spanish Civil War. The heroine, for instance, is a reversal of the typical lover of adventure novels. Described to us as a woman "fed up with kissing men," Palmera Suaretti uses and abuses her lovers to her own advantage. Jardiel sees her as a petty, selfish, irresponsible female, devoid of innocence but bored by romance. She is often the target of the author's misogynic comments about women and her role in the novel is therefore reduced to a level of scorn. Rarely do Jardiel's women suffer this indignity more than in his four novels; the heroines of his theater are by and large more engaging and believable.

Jardiel's digressions from his narrative into humorous parenthetical remarks, footnoted explanations, interpolated drawings, and frequent utterances to the reader are greatly stressed in this and his two subsequent novels. All such marginal trappings, while added to the narrative with an excess which at times delays the movement of the action, are a major ingredient of Jardiel's comic posture. Indeed, one discovers in his plethora of asides the sparkling originality of the author's novelistic technique. Whereas an occasional apostrophe or marginal notation would be deemed a peculiar if not unnecessary adornment in the style of most novelists, with Jardiel Poncela they are vital to the unfolding of his humor. The essence of his irony and criticism resides in the spontaneous comic outbursts which bespatter the pages of his prose, appearing frequently in the form of drawings, designs, cartoons, and signs, and elucidate with the humor of alliteration, antithesis, punning, and the mutation of word definitions the satire and colloquial discourse of his text.

Jardiel's affinity for cinematographic art is reflected repeatedly through the medium of pictorial illustrations in his novels. In *Siberia* he applies this technique again and again, offering the reader a graphic vision of the narrative action.[14] Lacosta sees in this practice a direct legacy from the surrealistic climate which influenced the artistic and literary expressions of the 1920's,[15] but Jardiel's vivid plasticity has little to do with the kind of subconscious dreamworld defined in the dictums of Breton, Apollinaire, and Guillermo de la Torre. His visual communications, wherein we detect an exuberance of comic sketches, framed announcements, and enlarged print repeating or inverting key words, are intended not only to amplify the reader's emotion, but more important, to provoke a humorous response beyond the surface amusement of the narrative. Jardiel's drawings are a reaffirmation of his comic inventiveness; they relate graphically to the reader's sense of hilarity in the same way that the theater spectator will respond to the visual humor enhanced by the movement and disposition of actors, furniture, props, and by the playwright's use of an unusual variety of settings.

Two examples will suffice to demonstrate to what extent Jardiel's drawings expand the textual possibilities of humor. When Mario visits Dr. Faber, he receives from the physician a written prescription of considerable length which is totally illegible. Jardiel reproduces the doctor's ungraceful script and offers us in turn his interpretation of that which baffles both the protagonist and the reader. Later on, Mario, in one of his many attempts at suicide, devours a handful of poisonous mushrooms. The author writes four times the word "mushrooms" (*setas*), doubling the size of the printed type with each repetition. Thus the reader is made aware, with a visual comic effect, of the hero's growing alarm and distending abdomen.

Jardiel often resorts to the device of diminishing or enlarging lines, signs, and words, or representing his drawings in a descending or ascending pattern, in order to convey the impression of a fade-in or fade-out of the camera or to enhance the reader's perception of physical movement. This is one of his innovative offerings to modern literature, a technique which carries the stamp of his own personality and of which he was proud to lay claim as the originator.

III   Eleven Thousand Virgins
(Pero . . . ¿hubo alguna vez once mil vírgenes?)

The task of writing his third novel, which he began during the first week of July, 1930, and completed in late November of that year, was briefly interrupted by a prolonged state of depression. Jardiel suffered occasional neurasthenic spells, periods during which he was oppressed with melancholy and despondency. The condition seemed to worsen as he grew older and in time it became the constant companion of his final years. On this occasion he sought to combat his depression by traveling northward to the cheerful countryside of the Basque provinces, where he regained some equanimity visiting the celebrated poetess and novelist Concha Espina. Then, turning south, he journeyed to the lovely surrounding of La Granja, where he spent several weeks restoring his confidence at the home of his friend and publisher, José Ruiz-Castillo. It was here at La Granja that he resumed writing the four hundred page novel, *Eleven Thousand Virgins*. Immediately following its publication, the novel provided an enormous financial return.

In his first two novels, Jardiel had parodied and satirized popular literary subjects. Once again he writes a travesty, but combines hostility with fun in order to deride a time-honored theme of world literature, the Don Juan myth. The hero of this new burlesque is named Pedro de Valdivia, a dashing young aristocrat whose exploits in the art of lovemaking, like those of the hero of Tirso, Molière, Zorrilla, and countless others, have become legendary. Pedro is orphaned at a tender age and soon finds himself under the tutelage of his Uncle Félix, a nonconforming bohemian who is determined to educate his nephew to become a consummate scoundrel. Uncle Félix sees himself as the only normal member of a degenerate family. Pedro's father, for instance, had been pathologically obsessed about washing his hands; his great-grandfather had spent an entire life carving the Gospels into the bark of trees. It is therefore Uncle Félix' sworn duty to dissociate Pedro from the family taint and to protect him from the peculiar ways of mankind by impressing upon his mind the importance of artifice and cunning. Pedro learns to detest society, to abhor marriage, and to distrust women. He is taught to blame others for his own losses and limitations. Thus, when Uncle Félix dies at the hands of an angry woman, Pedro swears vengeance on the entire female population of Spain, resolving to seduce with audacity as many women as come in contact with him and to abandon them afterwards with cold, calculated cruelty.

Following years of exciting conquests, Pedro becomes bored.

He has practiced every known stratagem of impertinence, has deceived thousands of women with his charm, and is now suddenly tired, listless, despondent. Then one evening, while drinking in an expensive cabaret, he meets Vivola Adamant, a brilliant, refined woman whose past record of seductions far surpasses Pedro's own history of amorous triumphs. She is his match in every way, but is as sated with loving men as he is in chasing after women. Despite his efforts to charm her, any seduction is impossible, and the two libertines part ways with a bond of friendship sealed by the disdain and boredom they share in common and a mutual respect for their differences. It is only after their parting that Pedro realizes he is in love with her—the only time in his debauched life that he has truly loved another human being.

Another character appears in the person of Luis Campa, a simple, innocent youngster who is eager to learn Pedro's famed methods with women. Luis's appeals finally prevail upon Pedro's ego, and the seasoned deceiver takes the boy into his confidence. Luis is amazed to learn that Valdivia is a highly sophisticated, professional profligate: he has carefully catalogued all of his conquests in an office file and is prepared to offer his advice concerning any conceivable amatory situation. Under the guidance of his mentor, Don Luis begins to blossom into a full-fledged Don Juan.

The action takes a sharp turn toward the crisis and denouement when a wealthy viscount proposes to leave Pedro two hundred thousand pesetas in exchange for Valdivia's ability to oblige a certain woman to marry the nobleman. Pedro accepts the bargain. In the company of his young apprentice, he goes to find his female victim. But to his awe and dismay, the woman is none other than Vivola Adamant, the very person he loves and fears above all females. His love-sick confusion so overwhelms him that he bungles the affair, disappointing himself, Vivola, the viscount, and Luis. With this failure Pedro is destroyed: morally, physically, and psychologically. To crown his defeat, Vivola eventually marries Luis, who successfully seduced her by utilizing the very lessons of audacity and cruelty he had learned from Pedro. In despair, Pedro de Valdivia turns to gambling, loses his fortune, and kills himself.

The author adds an appendix filled with humorous press releases reporting the demise of Pedro de Valdivia. One account states that a letter addressed to his servant was found in the suicide's pocket. Valdivia's servant had advised the libertine to marry a chaste girl and to settle down, but in his reply Pedro states categorically that there are no longer any virgins left in the world. He deploys several puns in mocking the words of an ancient religious allegory about eleven thousand virgins, adding his own stamp of skepticism to end the note. And thus the protagonist bequeaths to the reader a reason for the novel's unique title.

Jardiel's entertaining plot line, which shifts in and out of sarcasm and borders at times on the sardonic, combines a lively wit with a sustained parody of the exploits of an exalted archetypal hero. The author's choice to satirize Don Juan gives his writing a measure of interest far surpassing that of his other novels and accounts for the book's impressive commercial success. Pedro de Valdivia, as the parodied Don Juan figure, is, from the time of his pronounced boredom with women until his absurd death, the complete antithesis of the hero in the traditional myth. Jardiel portrays his libertine as a man whose negative qualities far outweigh his positive attributes, whose skeptical rejection of romantic love comes in conflict with latent sentimentality, resulting in the evolution of an emasculated lecher.

Valdivia's state of misery and emotional paralysis upon falling in love dispels our vision of the egocentric male figure commonly associated with the popular version of the Don Juan myth. It is one thing to tolerate the caricature of a legendary reprobate, and few of Don Juan's admirers in Spain will countenance the mutation of their hero from pursuer to inamorato;[16] but it is quite another matter to riddle that same caricature with burlesque, as Jardiel has done, reducing the humorous appeal of a love-sick malefactor to the level of the grotesque. When we encounter Pedro de Valdivia first attempting to seduce the woman he loves, then later importuning her favor on behalf of the viscount, our sense of compassion for his impotency, mingled with the hilarity we experience over his outrageous folly, produces a kind of comic catharsis, a farcical release of anxiety over Pedro's incompetency, leading to a fit of laughter concerning his impossible predicament. Discomfort gives way to amusement as a process of comic inversion takes place.[17] First we are led to laugh with the hero as he attacks the social order for its stupidity; then we are compelled to laugh at the man in his preposterous state as a Don Juan in love; and finally, we squirm with embarrassment but also laugh with glee at the sight of his collapse as he begs Vivola for some expression of love, and she refuses. Pedro's evolution from devil into clown, from the prototype of anarchy to the role of a deluded buffoon, climaxes a thematic triumph for Jardiel, but the true value of this narrative resides in the interrelation of protagonist and reader, that is, the psychological effect of the hero's comic plight on our sensibilities. The impact of this burlesque upon us is, as Eugenio de Nora states, "anything but cheerful," owing to its pessimistic tone.[18]

Jardiel's negative irony affords him the privilege of mocking the human condition through the triumphs and ultimate downfall of a protagonist who by his very nature and actions represents the scoffer (*el burlador*) of society's most cherished values. By transforming Pedro into a pitiable, tragicomic being, the antisocial thrust of Jardiel's treatment is not, however, reduced. For as the reader tends in the early chapters to identify with the deportment of the hero, following his every conquest with a sense of vicarious pleasure and reveling in the defiant manner by which he violates civil and moral laws, so in the later chapters the reader will find himself agreeing with the author's vitriolic criticisms on the ills of this world long after the hero's collapse; hence it is the novelist's cynical humor, not the protagonist's woes, which sustains the novel's social interest.

The novelist's rebellion is operative from the prologue to the appendix; he rebukes society before Pedro Valdivia's own antisocial bias takes shape and he censures the world long after his hero is debased. Three generations of reprobates preserve this rancor: Uncle Félix is his spokesman for anarchy, Valdivia instructs us in licentiousness, and Luis Campa, whose training as a Tenorio under Valdivia recalls the role of Luis Mejías in Zorrilla's play, represents the *fait accompli* of transgression's victory. It is he who outwits his teacher by winning the affections of the inaccessible Vivola Adamant, a woman whose curious name originates from the porcelain urinals on Madrid's public streets at the Puerta del Sol[19] and whose strength and intelligence in the novel stand in mock contrast to the meekness and passivity of other heroines in the long cycle of Don Juan productions. Vivola's strong, independent personality is equal in force to all three of the main male figures. Her role as a liberated female serves again to belittle the image of the conventional heroine in the popular literature of Jardiel's time.

IV   The Tour of God
(La "tournée" de Dios)

Jardiel's last novel is his most ambitious and, in many respects, his best published work. First conceived in the summer of 1929, *The Tour of God* was completed early in 1932. It brings together a large mass of disillusioned people, among them several characters from Jardiel's previous novels, in a kind of Jardielesque panorama of the human comedy. No one, however, stands out as a central hero or heroine. Jardiel assembles a large cross-section of society, including the Pope, several thieves, government leaders, and sexual perverts in a massive mockery of the human race. The intent of the novel is satirical, and the end result weighs heavily on the side of bitterness.

In his prologue Jardiel tries to disabuse his readers of their misjudging the novel as an antireligious tract. Its irreverence, he says, does not imply the denial of his feeling for the divine. It is rather the result of his profound skepticism vis-à-vis the human condition. *The Tour of God*, Jardiel insists, is an attack on humanity, not on the church or deity.

Book One begins with the earthshaking announcement from the Pope that God plans to visit Spain. This important news item is first made public by Perico Espasa, the director of a large metropolitan newspaper and a man whose personal life is enshrouded in homosexual activities; and by Federico Orellana, an important novelist who has a very ill son, the illegitimate fruit of a love affair with a beautiful actress. When the two men promulgate the news of the Pope's vision, the entire

world ridicules their message. The Pope, in the meantime, receives a second vision. On this occasion God informs
His Holiness that, in order to convince a disbelieving world,
He will show a sign of His coming by destroying and then re-
constructing the leaning tower of Pisa. The world awaits the
event in a spirit of subdued mockery. When the miracle is
indeed performed, all human beings frantically dedicate them-
selves to adoring and worshiping the Supreme Being.

Book Two describes the Lord's visit. Spain is His first choice
because it is the one nation that has fought hardest and longest
for His cause. He plans to appear on the Cerro de los Angeles,
the exact geographical center of Spain. At the appointed hour,
a gigantic crowd presses close around the hill, awaiting God's
arrival with more fear than shame. A moment of silent stupor
greets His appearance. Then the crowd suddenly advances,
pushing, shoving, and shouting with such unchecked fury that
the Spanish Guardia Civil is obliged to open fire on the multitudes to protect God from physical abuse. Thousands of people
are crushed or slaughtered in the holocaust, an awesome,
ironic spectacle of blood and horror which displays the ugly
ramifications of a rebellion of the masses.

In the wake of the Cerro de los Angeles disaster, God's wel-
coming party hurries Him off to the capital for a historical interview with Perico Espasa. The divine interview is completely
unsatisfactory: God gives mysterious, ambiguous answers to
every question. In the meantime, all hell breaks loose on earth.
Absolute social disorder prevails: No one works, everybody
plays. The world is in turmoil. Finally, God decides to speak
in public, to calm the multitudes in their craze over His visit.

He selects the Madrid bullring as a suitable spot for his
public discourse. This is the high point of the novel, the apex
of Jardiel's ironic humor and the crux of his bitterness. In his
speech to the world, God accuses humanity of such selfishness
that the Supreme Being has been driven to live in eternal soli-
tude. As was the case with His Son, God's aloneness is assured
by humanity's indifference. He will therefore refuse to satisfy
His creatures as to His divine will or their need to know all
the answers. His oration is delivered with firmness, but in a
tone of melancholy and despair.

In the final part of *The Tour of God*, Perico Espasa, responding to the insistence of Federico Orellana, asks the Lord to intervene on behalf of Federico's ill son. God promises to do all He can in his mortal role. He visits the boy, gives him an injection, and the boy dies. Both Perico and Federico are abashed over the Lord's failure to save the youngster. As a consequence, God loses His last friends. Misunderstood and hated owing to the same blind egoism which destroyed His Son, the Lord, in sadness, departs the earth.

The author's bitter accusations center repeatedly on the stupidity, selfishness, and imbalance of human concerns. The bittersweet humor he employs to lash out at immorality and to laugh at the ridiculous state of mankind is reminiscent of Mariano José de Larra, the nineteenth-century Spanish satirist, and of Pío Baroja, the great twentieth-century novelist, both of whom Jardiel admired. The author's impulse to span all social levels, attempting to counsel and mortify the human race, recalls the pessimistic humor and social intent of Mateo Alemán's celebrated picaresque tale, *Guzmán de Alfarache*. Yet this presentation of an unhinged, disjointed world fraught with tragicomic riddles and frivolous functions, teeming with laughable incongruities, is typically and uniquely the product of Jardiel Poncela's craft. He juggles his narrative line with carnivalesque dexterity, moving from the scornful thrust of sarcasm to the gentle caress of irony, shifting from a caustic denunciation of all mankind to a conciliatory indulgence with his individual characters. As one begins to tire under the weight of derision, Jardiel's sneers suddenly merge into merriment. And before laughter can assume full command, his humor will give way again to asperity.

This special affiliation of mirth with mockery confers a unique stamp of originality on Jardiel's writing. His best efforts to achieve unusual and startling effects, demonstrated in the structure, characterization, and language of his novels and plays, meet with particular success in *The Tour of God*. Part of this achievement is due to the sustained fun he has with his readers, mixing moral judgments with immoral pronouncements, ridiculing people with a tongue-in-cheek capriciousness which suggests a literary indebtedness to Oscar Wilde, George Bernard Shaw, and Pittigrilli. Part is also due to the continuous contact he maintains with the reader, utilizing graphics, signs, cartoons, annotations, and parenthetical remarks to heighten the impact of his sportive satire and to deform many of the human qualities of his characters by emphasizing the sterility and emptiness of their lives. In this respect, Jardiel's final novel brings to mind the possible influence of Ramón Gómez de la Serna and Luigi Pirandello, each of whom had a decisive sway on Jardiel's choice of themes and development of style throughout a good part of his literary endeavors.[20]

The Tour of God contains several disquieting passages. The most awesome episode is the mass murder of thousands of Spaniards by the armed guards who preside over God's initial appearance. This was written in 1932. The events of Spain of four years later now cast a hue of prophetic horror on Jardiel's description of the holocaust. Another ominous section is found in the Preface, wherein Jardiel speaks of humanity having lost confidence in itself, having surrendered its healthy perspective to run headlong into total bankruptcy. Aside from the stentorian laughter the novel frequently evokes, and beyond its many witty quips, *The Tour of God* is intended to elicit an occasional sober and startling reflection on man and his God.

CHAPTER 5

Jardiel's Position and Influence Today

ASIDE from his legacy of a surface comicity that has its unique appeal in surprise of action and complication of plot; aside from his farcical development of unusual characters and the disclosure of a fast, witty, unexpected dialogue; and aside from his manifestation of outrageous absurdity and the startling use of technical devices, what were Jardiel Poncela's contributions to the literature of our day? He had set out, as early as 1927, "to renew and to elevate" Spanish humor, both in the novel and in the theater. Did he in fact succeed? Is today's theater or novel any different, any better, or any worse because of his efforts to change its course?

I Nature and Importance of Jardiel's Innovations

If we give credence to the opinions of his disciples and present-day admirers, there is no doubt that Jardiel left the theater, rather than the novel, enriched by his verve and imagination, his exuberance and daring. He electrified its tired old reliance on insipid domestic farce by his dizzying pace and flamboyant histrionics. He inspired an entire generation of dramatists to probe beyond a facile level of slapstick for new comic effects based on a sophisticated complication of plot and the intelligent use of repartee. Clearly, not all playwrights of the comic genre have followed his example, but he left them that example nonetheless.

Because Jardiel exercised little reflective judgment or introspection into the profundities of human nature, his name has been ignored by those European and American critics who generally overlook Spain altogether when seeking authentic purveyors of the avant-garde or theater of the absurd in Western literature. Yet an absurdist he was. His themes, of course,

94

do not pertain in general to existential despair or the psychic annihilation of the individual. Except perhaps for the last of his four novels, wherein he is apparently concerned about the fate of mankind in a world filled with hypocrisy and evil, Jardiel has little sense of anguish at the disintegration of man in a society bereft of cosmic values. But his extravagant departures from logic, the incongruity of his language, and the surprising concatenation of unpredictable scenes, bring him well within the tradition of a typically Spanish dimension of the absurd, that area wherein twentieth-century writers from Enrique García Álvarez to Miguel Mihura have employed deviation, incoherence, and incongruity to combat the banality and dullness of everyday communication. Jardiel's theater achieves the kind of liberating effect that Martin Esslin refers to when he says that an absurd play should expand the limits of sense and open up vistas of freedom from logic and cramping convention.[1] It is in his attitude towards language and action—that is, his use of verbal nonsense and mad, irrational happenings to point out the insufficiency, the sterility, and the stupidity of commonplace stage humor—that Jardiel is most revolutionary. He transcended the mawkish, methodical manner of Pedro Muñoz Seca's approach to the absurd, only to be surpassed by the more intellectual type of absurd humor demonstrated by Miguel Mihura in his early plays. But it is Jardiel who keeps alive and provocative the line of the bizarre in Spanish theater humor; he links the unsophisticated past to the more discerning luster of the modern era without descending for too long a stay into the arena of frivolous pop literature. His technical skills lifted nonsense from the plane of wild caricature to a level of solid construction, melding the improbable with an occasional serious tone and a timely poetic vein. The energy by which he demanded so much of himself to bring this about had far greater an impact and influence on his contemporaries and followers than did his actual accomplishments. Sadly, his creative genius was all too frequently arrested by superficial predilections, his inventiveness crippled by an unrestrained exuberance in plot and language, his own peace of mind ravaged by despair and possibly by paranoia. Yet the man's indefatigable energy and idealism offered a degree of compensation for his unrealized intentions, and this alone injected new life and vigor into the Spanish theater.

Some of the theater innovations Jardiel prized most highly are not often cited with his name. He brought, for instance, several cinematographic techniques to the legitimate theater that he had developed in his Hollywood film work, namely, the simultaneous use of multiple scenes, filmed background, and diverse lighting experiments with varied use of scrims. The total effect of these advances was to add rapidity and variety to stage action.

II *Current Judgments*

A new generation of playgoers and drama critics has replaced the audiences of Jardiel's time. The audacious innovations propounded on the far more liberal stage of today's Spanish theater —compared, of course, to the conservative blandness of the first half of the twentieth century—overshadow the thrust and brilliance of Jardiel's daring experiments with theme and humor. The national furor once engendered by his most eccentric creative productions has now become a quaint and palatable phenomenon of literary history. His talent and imagination are still heralded in an occasional doctoral thesis, but his name has been relegated to a back shelf in the old curiosity shop of Spanish drama.

Yet few will deny the authenticity of Jardiel's role as pioneer. His plays are now rarely performed, but most of today's prominent playwrights and critics (within Spain) declare their unwavering indebtedness to his example. To their minds, the theater of Enrique Jardiel Poncela is synonymous with the notion of a new departure, a bold endeavor, a hard-fought beginning, for which they are now the benefactors. Lauro Olmo, for instance, one of Spain's most important contemporary playwrights, lauds Jardiel's "struggle for freedom of idea and expression" and "his example as an author in search of that which is original, surprising, and inverisimilar. His achievements presupposed the existence of windows through which a renewing and necessary fresh breeze could enter—and still enters—for the benefit of comic expression in the Spanish theater."[2] According to Adolfo Prego, a drama critic assigned to Madrid's *ABC* and *Blanco y Negro*, "the Spanish theater of humor would be entirely different were it not for Jardiel's titanic struggle . . . to widen the horizons of comedy." Like Lauro Olmo, Prego considers Jardiel's most significant contribution to be the playwright's unflagging devotion to challenge the adversaries of free dramatic expression: "For Jardiel the theater was a constant spectacle, that is to say, from the time the curtain went up until the denouement occurred, each and every scene had a value of its own in the author's mind." He imposed on every theme and action "a freedom of focus and treatment unimpaired by the long literary tradition of conventional logic."[3]

Angel Laborda, Prego's colleague on the staff of *ABC*, enlarges upon the idea that Jardiel's form of logic was incompatible with that of his contemporaries: "Madrid was accustomed to a natural theater, to a classical order in the development of dramatic action, to palpable and recognizable characters, to a slow rhythm of performances—and Jardiel destroyed it all!" Laborda believes that all of Jardiel's surprising innovations, rejected by the theatergoing public over thirty years ago, have now triumphed in the writings of lesser talent, but only because Jardiel gave to those innovations a magnetic impetus which led to their inevitable acceptance. Laborda calls for a revaluation of and a renewed interest in "an active staging of his best plays. Jardiel Poncela should now receive the admiration he enjoyed before the [Spanish Civil] War and which the postwar scene denied him. . . . His vitality, his enormous energy, must not be relegated to mere reading."[4]

Not all current judgments focus on Jardiel's achievements in the theater. Antonio Valencia, who wrote the preface to the latest edition of Jardiel's most popular novel, *The Tour of God*, believes that Jardiel's full potential as a fine novelist was never realized, that he made a grave error in renouncing narrative fiction, a genre that "would have brought him more lasting fame and literary importance" than the theater.[5]

For the dramatist Antonio Buero Vallejo, Jardiel will, in the course of time, be accorded the status of a "true classic writer" of the Spanish stage, one whose sense of "magic" more than of "logic" is evident in his best plays. But Jardiel was obliged, states Buero, to become more "an original craftsman than a poet, simply because his public persuaded him to revel in trivial jokes and comic effects. But craftsmanship also has formidable theater value when it is applied to the service of felicitous ideas and situations. Jardiel was, above all, a successful creator of ideas and unusual situations, and in that sense, he was a great renovator. Mihura and Ionesco would come after him and would perhaps do it better, but Jardiel came first."[6]

One distinguished writer no longer shares Buero's enthusiasm for Jardiel's role. Alfonso Sastre, acclaimed by many critics as Spain's most important contemporary dramatist, agrees that Jardiel's "comic imagination surpassed that of his many incompetent and mediocre colleagues," but Sastre insists that, in the main, his theater "is terribly shallow" and contains no more than "a kind of mechanical comicity that makes it anachronous today," relying as it does on pure laughter and reflecting Jardiel's "disregard for political and historical issues. Personally, though," writes Sastre, "he taught me matters of the trade and, above all, to love theater work."[7]

Perhaps the harshest judgment on Jardiel's theater was uttered in April of 1972 by Miguel Mihura, the man most often cited as Jardiel Poncela's successor in the Spanish theater of humor.[8] According to Mihura, Jardiel's theater "is a pirouette, an impermanent, inconsequential thing that has no relevance in today's world. The recent resurgence of a few Jardiel plays is merely in honor to his memory, not the result of popular interest. No one really understands his theater. His language and characters, like those of Carlos Arniches before him, are too Madrilenean to be appreciated beyond the nation's capital." But Mihura concedes that the theater public is no more ready for Jardiel's audacity now than it was thirty years ago. With characteristic cynicism, Mihura affirms that "Jardiel's theater will never be understood."[9] Francisco García Pavón, the theater critic for *Arriba*, is an admirer of Jardiel's theater, but he concurs with Mihura's statement that Jardiel Poncela's writings are still beyond the grasp of Spanish playgoers, in that it remains "superior to the average intelligence of his public."[10]

What is the current opinion of those who knew Jardiel personally? Most of his friends and associates heap a cascade of lavish encomiums on his memory. José María Pemán, for example, born only three years before Jardiel, recalls his old friend with a sense of fond nostalgia. He views Jardiel's legacy as constituting "a perfect synthesis of humor and tenderness."[11] Joaquín Calvo Sotelo likewise celebrates "the easy, graceful delivery of his audacity, the originality of selected themes, and the immense and vibrating vital joy that traversed and gave life to all of his prodigious labor."[12] Other opinions expressed by several of Jardiel's close associates, such as José López Rubio (with whom Jardiel collaborated in their early cinematographic achievements) and Alfonso Paso (who was married for a time to Jardiel's daughter, Evangelina), are of a similar positive vein.

Another of Jardiel's contemporaries, the uncompromising defender of *Jardielismo* in Spain, Alfredo Marqueríe, maintains that the influence of his theater has never waned nor ever will: "It lives on in many of the plays of Edgar Neville, José López Rubio, Joaquín Calvo Sotelo, Miguel Mihura, Tono, Álvaro de Laiglesia, Alfonso Paso, Carlos Llopis, and Juan José Alonso Millán."[13] Marqueríe insists that "the majority of Jardiel's plays will always remain in the anthology of Iberian theater humor. Some of them are merely circumstantial and will probably be forgotten, but others, wherein Jardiel approaches, in a comic manner, profound problems of the human condition, of love and of society," these, Marqueríe affirms, "will never be erased."[14] Jardiel's highly regarded vindicator sums up his favorable judgment of the playwright by listing these notable achievements in the course of his dramatic career:

Humorous situations carried to the extreme, the depiction of eccentric and extravagant characters, the thematic incorporation of the impossible and the wondrous, a mockery of the commonplace and of the small bourgeois society with all of its hypocrisies and prejudices, the detective tale treated comically, mystery mingled with the macabre, the use of insanity to contrast with a panorama that only appears to be sane, and, finally, a highly ingenious colloquial game of unanticipated and surprising retorts or of contrasting attitudes, together with sophisms of an irresistible hilarity.[15]

If the theater of Jardiel Poncela is still a vigorous force in the Spanish theater world, as Marqueríe and Jardiel's other admirers unhesitatingly assert, why then are his plays, aside from an infrequent revival of three or four of his best-known titles, no longer performed? The answer lies in the simple explanation that, economically speaking, they are no longer performable. Jardiel's theater presents acute "material difficulties that arise from the complexities of staging and from the fact that an extraordinary number of actors are required by the casting."[16] Even Marquerie admits that the physical assembly of his plays militates against a successful revival.[17] Today's economic pressures within the theater arts oblige the director to reduce severely his use of props, stage hands, scenery, and the cast of characters. Jardiel Poncela's theater, which requires an exceptional overabundance of all these needs, is far too costly a phenomenon for present-day staging. Owing to their great demands for a full company, his plays also require a full house of spectators to pay the bills. His theater still presents the director with the greatest financial risk in modern Spanish history. If Mihura's skeptical opinion is true—that the public cannot understand Jardiel and will not attend his plays—and the cost factor continues to be decisive, it seems reasonable to predict that the theater of Enrique Jardiel Poncela will simply remain a matter of historical curiosity for some time to come.

Notes and References

Chapter One

1. Juan Bonet Gelabert, *El discutido indiscutible Jardiel Poncela* (Madrid: Biblioteca Nueva, 1946).

2. Rafael Flórez, *Mío Jardiel* (Madrid: Biblioteca Nueva, 1966) and *Jardiel Poncela* (Madrid: EPESA, 1969).

3. Evangelina Jardiel Poncela intends to publish a book about her father when her present series of articles entitled "Así era mi padre," appearing in various issues of the Madrid journal, *Sábado Gráfico,* is concluded.

4. Evangelina Jardiel Poncela, in a letter directed to the Spanish novelist, Miguel Delibes, reveals the origin of the family's surnames: "Jardiel is a Hebrew name (Jar: energy; di: of; and El: abbreviation of Elohim: God) . . . The first Jardiels must have arrived in Spain after the Inquisition . . . The surname first appeared at Quinto del Ebro (Zaragoza). Poncela is likewise an Italian Jewish name, and when it was Hispanicized, it lost one 'l.' " See Miguel Delibes, *Un año de mi vida* (Barcelona: Destino, 1972), pp. 94–95.

5. See "8986 palabras a manera de prólogo," in Enrique Jardiel Poncela, *Obras completas,* IV (Barcelona: Editorial AHR, 1965), 1193–1217.

6. These juvenile writings were produced, for the most part, at the family's farm in Quinto del Ebro, Zaragoza, where Jardiel spent every summer. His mother destroyed all of his adolescent literature when the family moved to its new flat at Number 15 Churruca Street in 1916.

7. A few titles that Jardiel wrote during this period (1919–1925) were published in several Madrid periodicals, among them *El Imparcial, Los Lunes,* and the weekly magazine, *Buen Humor.* In this latter publication, Jardiel's style seems to crystalize, about 1922, as a strong vein of humor replaces the light romantic inclination of his earlier writings.

8. Ramón Gómez de la Serna (1888–1963), the creator of the imperishable *greguería,* a humorous statement structured on metaphor, paradox, or logical dissociation, was the undisputed leader of the so-called Café Literature Generation, whose members frequented

bohemian *tertulia* gatherings and produced exciting, provocative, nihilistic humor. Wenceslao Fernández Flórez (1885–1964) was a major figure in the promotion of the humor of irony, social bitterness, and a daring skepticism that occasionally bordered on sarcasm and pessimism. Other members of this generation included Joaquín Belda (1880?–1937), who specialized in erotic literature; Julio Camba (1882–1962), whose travel literature and journalistic observations added a mellow, cosmopolitan strain, reminiscent of Chesterton, to the humor of this period; and the incomparable Ramón del Valle-Inclán (1886–1935), whose eccentric life style and devotion to theatrical caricature earned him a blend of international recognition and local notoriety.

9. The plays were never produced. Their titles are *A Reputable Man* (*Un hombre de bien*) and *The Year 2500* (*El año 2500*), written in 1924 and 1925, respectively.

10. Jardiel's commitments from 1926 through the first of his two short residences in Hollywood (1932) included an outstanding number of activities. He wrote dozens of articles and short narratives for at least fourteen different periodicals; he gave two broadcasts per month on Madrid's Union Radio; he wrote two long novels, five novelettes, and published *Pirulís de la Habana* (Madrid: Editorial Popular, 1927), a collection of miscellaneous short writings; he staged three of his own full-length plays and several sketches, some in collaboration; he prepared the dialogue and screen adaptation for Carlos Arniches's *That's My Man* (*Es mi hombre*), in a film version directed by Fernández Cuenca; and he delivered numerous lectures on humorous topics, especially about women and sex.

11. This book consists of many anecdotes of Jardiel's association with Catalina Bárcena, Gregorio Martínez Sierra, José López Rubio, and Julio Peña, among others who constituted his closely-knit Spanish colony in Hollywood.

12. José Ruiz-Castillo, who edited Jardiel's collection of lectures, early short stories, and miscellaneous essays under the title *Excess Baggage* (*Exceso de equipaje*), was the first to recognize the novelty and popularity of this new art form. His praise for Jardiel did much to solidify the playwright's reputation as an innovator in the field of cinematic art.

13. The silent films included in this series were "The Great Train Robbery" (1903), "The Heart of Waleska" (1905), "Twin Dukes and a Duchess" (1905), "Emma's Dilemma" (1906), "For the Man She Loved" (1907), and "The Chorus Girl" (1908).

14. See Jardiel's prologues to *Cuatro corazones con freno y*

marcha atrás and *Los ladrones somos gente honrada*, in *Obras completas* (Barcelona: AHR, 1965), I, 847–75 and II, 155–81. Hammarstrand suggests that "it is entirely possible that the reaction to Jardiel's very positive [political] declarations may have acerbated the opposition to his later works." See Robert Edward Hammarstrand, *The Comic Spirit in the Plays of Enrique Jardiel Poncela* (University of California, Berkeley, 1966), Doctoral thesis, p. 26.

15. The tour played in Salamanca, Palencia, Valladolid, Pamplona, San Sebastián, Bilbao, and Santander.

16. Jardiel's blanket condemnation of all critics, "the living aberration of literature," as he called them, did not include Alfredo Marqueríe, the one writer he admired above all others "for objective, honest reporting," which meant Marqueríe's unwavering praise for Jardiel's efforts.

17. Alberto Canay expends a considerable amount of time and effort developing this thesis. See his *Recuerdo y presencia de Enrique Jardiel Poncela* (Buenos Aires: Edición del autor, 1958).

18. One example of Jardiel's vendetta against particular individuals is found in his so-called "Contradedicatoria," or "Anti-Dedication," to his collection of plays, *Agua, aceite y gasolina y otras dos mezclas explosivas*, in which the playwright names seven critics as having "inflicted the greatest injustice possible on a sensible, honest, and sincere artist." See *Obras*, II, 599.

19. See "Ensayo sobre el teatro español," in *Obras*, I, 83–150.

20. Information conveyed in a personal interview with Miguel Mihura, April 26, 1972.

21. See Mariluz Jardiel Poncela, "Enrique Jardiel Poncela," in *Teatro*, No. 4 (Madrid: February, 1953), pp. 27–28; Evangelina Jardiel Poncela, "Prólogo a tres comedias escogidas," in Enrique Jardiel Poncela, *Obras*, II, 933–37.

22. Personal contacts made by the writer of this study in April of 1972.

23. Canay, pp. 26, 105–11.

24. Personal letter to the writer of this study, dated October 22, 1973.

25. Jardiel Poncela, *Obra inédita* (Barcelona: AHR, 1967), p. 359.

26. Hammarstrand, pp. 28–29.

Chapter Two

1. As recalled by Rafael Flórez, *Mío Jardiel* (Madrid: Biblioteca Nueva, 1966), p. 60.

2. Alberto Canay, *Recuerdo y presencia de Enrique Jardiel Poncela* (Buenos Aires: Edición del autor, 1958), p. 33.

3. Juan Bonet Gelabert, *El discutido indiscutible Jardiel Poncela* (Madrid: Biblioteca Nueva, 1946), pp. 209–29.

4. Flórez, pp. 69–72.

5. *Ibid.*, pp. 64 and 67.

6. Bonet, p. 28.

7. Flórez, p. 123.

8. Quoted in Phyllis Z. Boring, *The Bases of Humor in the Conemporary Spanish Theatre* (Gainesville: University of Florida doctoral thesis, 1966), p. 39.

9. Alfredo Marqueríe, "Novedad en el teatro de Jardiel," in J. Rof Carballo *et al.*, *El teatro de humor en España* (Madrid: Editora Nacional, 1966), p. 72.

10. *Ibid.*, p. 69.

11. *Ibid.*, p. 75.

12. Enrique Jardiel Poncela, *Obras completas*, I (Barcelona: Editorial AHR, 1965), 163.

13. Canay, p. 34.

14. Quoted in Bonet, p. 71.

15. Jardiel Poncela, *Obras completas*, I, 232–33.

16. See "La última entrevista," in *Teatro: Revista Internacional de la Escena*, No. 5 (Madrid: February, 1953), p. 30.

17. The first act was, in fact, so well liked that it received a standing ovation and the author was summoned to take a bow. By the middle of Act Three, however, the audience ended its sustained period of whistling and footstamping by deserting the theater en masse. See Jardiel Poncela, *Obras completas*, I, 229.

18. Flórez, p. 166.

19. Jardiel, *Obras completas*, I, 305.

20. Nicolás González Ruiz, for example, an avowed anti-Jardielist, credited this work as being "the most perfect of all his plays." (See his *La cultura española en los últimos veinte años: El teatro* [Madrid: Instituto de Cultura Hispánica, 1949], p. 28). Such has been the judgment imposed upon *Margarita, Armando and His Father* by almost all of those critics who normally disdain Jardiel's theater.

21. Bonet, p. 69.

22. See Jardiel, *Obras completas*, I, 568.

23. Jardiel's novels are discussed in Chapter 4 of this study.

24. Flórez, p. 180.

25. Boring, p. 43.

26. Enrique Díez-Canedo, *Artículos de crítica teatral: El teatro*

español de 1914 a 1936, IV (México: Joaquín Mortiz, 1968), 260–61.

27. Alfredo Marqueríe, *Veinte años de teatro en España* (Madrid: Editora Nacional, 1959), p. 67.

28. Alfredo Marqueríe, "Novedad en el teatro de Jardiel," in J. Rof Carballo *et al., op. cit.,* p. 72.

29. See, for instance, González Ruiz, *op. cit.,* p. 28.

30. Rafael Flórez, *Jardiel Poncela* (Madrid: EPESA, 1969), pp. 29, 98, and 105.

31. Jardiel Poncela, *Obras completas,* I, 753.

32. Rafael Flórez, *Jardiel Poncela,* pp. 97 and 105.

33. Díez-Canedo, *op. cit.,* I, 44.

34. The three d'Orsian commentaries from *El Debate* are reproduced in their entirety in Chapter 24 of Rafael Flórez, *Mío Jardiel* (Madrid: Biblioteca Nueva, 1966), pp. 213–20.

35. Flórez, *Mío Jardiel,* p. 222.

36. Jardiel Poncela, *Obras completas,* I, 388–89.

37. Francisco Ruiz Ramón, *Historia del teatro español,* 2 (Madrid: Alianza Editorial, 1971), p. 308.

38. Francisco García Pavón, *Textos y escenarios* (Barcelona: Plaza y Janes, S.A., Editores, 1971), pp. 96 and 105.

39. *Ibid.,* p. 104.

Chapter Three

1. Juan Emilio Aragonés, *Teatro español de posguerra* (Madrid: Publicaciones Españoles Núm. 520, 1971), p. 10.

2. As one example, the household furnishings required for the opening scene of Act One include a sixteenth-century canopy bed, an enormous well-stocked bookcase, a bar, a grand piano and four music racks, three sofas, six armchairs, five or six period chairs, four or five large tables, three or four consoles, two or three chests of drawers, many chairs, a gigantic brazier, crocks, clocks, lamps, pots, urns, statues, vases, a railroad station bell, firearms, playthings, a microscope, a violin, a saxophone, a guitar, a roulette wheel, a typewriter, a pair of dueling pistols, etc., etc. The list, to be complete, would require another page of enumerated items. See Jardiel Poncela, *Obras completas,* I, 1259–61.

3. Gonzalo Torrente Ballester, *Teatro español contemporáneo* (Madrid: Guadarrama, 1957), pp. 255–56.

4. Francisco Ruiz Ramón, *Historia del teatro español,* 2 (Madrid: Alianza Editorial, 1971), 306.

5. Nicolás González Ruiz, *La cultura española en los últimos*

veinte años: El teatro (Madrid: Instituto de Cultura Hispánica, 1949), pp. 27–28.

6. Jardiel Poncela, *Obras completas*, I, 1106.

7. Quoted by Alfredo Marqueríe, "Novedad en el teatro de Jardiel," in Juan Rof Carballo, *et al., El teatro de humor en Enspaña* (Madrid: Editora Nacional, 1966), p. 77.

8. Jardiel Poncela, *Obra inédita* (Barcelona: AHR, 1967), p. 316.

9. Fernández de Asís, in *Pueblo* (Madrid, February 21, 1946), p. 4.

10. Mihura has further related that his disagreement with Jardiel came about for personal reasons related to borrowing money. On such matters, Mihura declared, "Jardiel was vain, irritable, and rancorous." Information conveyed in a personal interview with Miguel Mihura, April 26, 1972.

11. Ruiz Ramón, pp. 307–8.

12. Alfredo Marqueríe, *Veinte años de teatro en España* (Madrid: Editora Nacional, 1959), p. 66.

13. The story's original title was "Imagination's Power" ("El poder de la imaginación"). See Jardiel Poncela, *Obras completas*, II, 157.

14. *Ibid.*, p. 181.

15. Alfredo Marqueríe, *El teatro de Jardiel Poncela* (Bilbao: Ediciones de Conferencias y Ensayos, 1945), p. 15.

16. Jardiel, *Obras completas*, II, 181.

17. Alfredo Marqueríe, "Novedad en el teatro de Jardiel," in J. Rof Carballo, *et al., op. cit.*, p. 77.

18. Adolfo Prego, "Crítica teatral sobre *Tú y yo somos tres*," in *ABC* (Madrid, April 8, 1972), pp. 87–88.

19. See note 15 above.

20. *Ibid.*, pp. 40 and 46.

21. Juan Bonet Gelabert, *El discutido indiscutible Jardiel Poncela* (Madrid: Biblioteca Nueva, 1946), p. 157.

22. Jardiel left the following comment about this undertaking: "In 1932, having lived in Hollywood for some nine or ten months, working as a film writer for Fox in the company of Pepe López Rubio, and by then knowing well the city and its customs, I conceived the idea of writing a play about the fabric of that existence, at once both brilliant and miserable, seductive and frightening, simple and preposterous, infantile and satanical, ... and overflowing with the attraction and hypnotism of the unexpected." See *Obras completas*, II, 11.

23. Jardiel seemed obsessed with the idea of amassing physical props for this production. With an effort to present faithfully the

behind-the-scenes life of "authentic" Hollywood, he lists two pages of objects that he insisted be included in the stage settings for *Love Lasts Only 2000 Meters.*

24. See Jardiel's "Prólogo a la comedia: lo moral y lo inmoral," in *Obras completas,* II, 283–89.

25. See Jardiel's Introduction to *3 proyectiles del 42,* in *Obras completas,* II, 275.

26. The same theme was treated 111 years earlier by Bretón de los Herreros in his *Marcela, o ¿cuál de los tres?*

27. See Jardiel's "Prólogo a *Los habitantes de la casa deshabitada:* Lo vulgar y lo inverosímil," in *Obras completas,* II, p. 500.

28. Marqueríe writes that *The Cat's Seven Lives* "demonstrates how possible it is to do the impossible, that is, to mix tragedy and the grotesque, drama and humor, reality and fantasy, logic and absurdity, without allowing the work to lose its line of harmony." See Alfredo Marqueríe's theater review of the play reproduced in Jardiel Poncela, *Obras completas,* II, 503–7.

29. Alfredo Marqueríe, "Novedad en el teatro de Jardiel," in J. Rof Carballo, *et al., op. cit.,* p. 80.

30. *Ibid.,* "Crítica de la comedia *El pañuelo de la dama errante,*" in Jardiel Poncela, *Obras completas,* II, 704.

31. See Rafael Flórez, "Cronología," in *Jardiel Poncela* (Madrid: EPESA, 1969), p. 184.

32. Jardiel's overreaction is evinced by the self-criticism he wrote in a detailed analysis of the play's highly-publicized fizzle. See *Obras completas,* II, pp. 803–16.

33. This annual award is conferred by the Spanish Consejo Superior del Teatro.

34. Rafael Flórez, *Mío Jardiel* (Madrid: Biblioteca Nueva, 1966), p. 326.

35. See Jardiel Poncela, *Obras completas,* II, 926.

36. Evangelina Jardiel Poncela states that a number of spectators were seen to be testing their whistles before entering the theater, predisposed to begin a protest within. The play, she claims, was an enormous success in spite of those who insisted on its failure. See Jardiel Poncela, *Obras completas,* II, 926–27.

Chapter Four

1. Some biographies list *The Astral Plane (El plano astral)* of 1922 as Jardiel's first novel. However, this publication is only fifty-three pages long and belongs more appropriately among the titles of

his many short novels. It is found in Jardiel Poncela, *Obras completas*, IV (Barcelona: AHR, 1965), 1261–1341.

2. Jardiel contributed to such magazines and journals as *Blanco y Negro, Buen Humor, La Correspondencia de España, Gutiérrez, La Libertad, El Libro Galante, La Novela de Amor, La Novela Deportiva, La Novela Vivida, Los Novelistas, Nuestra Novela, Nuevo Mundo, Los Once*, and *Ondas*, among others. His unpublished works of fiction, like many of his repudiated plays, have been consigned to an everlasting oblivion, but not destroyed, at the author's request.

3. See Jardiel Poncela, *Obras completas*, IV, 1216–17.

4. That Jardiel's satiric shock treatment may have scandalized his reading public and, ironically, may have contributed to the very current he possibly wished to combat, is suggested by Juan Bonet, who states that the book's popular success was due largely to its "most daring pages." See Juan Bonet Gelabert, *El discutido indiscutible Jardiel Poncela* (Madrid: Biblioteca Nueva, 1946), p. 49.

5. Bonet (*op. cit.*, p. 49) would disagree with this evaluation. He insists that the "supreme charm of Jardiel's wit" destroyed once and for all the readers' capacity to read erotic novels seriously! With this argument Bonet claims that Jardiel did indeed destroy a genre of subliterature and did indeed fulfill his prefatory pledge.

6. Jean Lorrain (1855–1906) and Rachilde (b. 1862) have now passed into literary oblivion. They first made their reputation by novels of the perverse.

7. Realism and sensuality prevail in the very popular early novels of Insúa (1833–1963) and López de Haro (b. 1876). Hoyos y Vinent (1886–1940) likewise began his writing career under the decadent sway of Rachilde, while Zamacois (b. 1873) has the distinction of being the first Spanish novelist to cultivate the French erotic novel, an honor falsely attributed to Felipe Trigo (1864–1916), who has carried much of the blame for the entire explosion of crudity and sensualism in the modern Spanish novel.

8. Federico Carlos Sainz de Robles, *La novela corta española* (Madrid: Aguilar, 1952), pp. 27–28.

9. See "El tema sexual de la literatura," in Pío Baroja, *Obras completas* (Madrid: Biblioteca Nueva, 1948), p. 926.

10. Julio Cejador y Frauca, *Historia de la lengua y literatura castellana*, XIII (Madrid: Publicaciones de la Revista de Arch., Bibl. y Museos, 1920), 19.

11. Eugenio de Nora, *La novela española contemporánea*, II (Madrid: Gredos, 1958–62), 250.

12. Francisco Lacosta Cebollada, *Enrique Jardiel Poncela: El*

humorismo en su novela (University of Missouri, 1966). Doctoral thesis, p. 163.

13. Alberto Canay, *Recuerdo y presencia de Enrique Jardiel Poncela* (Buenos Aires: Edición del autor, 1958), p. 34.

14. The importance of the reader's response to visual impressions is made clear by Guillermo de Torre: "The reader must create by means of sight a special system of comprehension. His drawing-image carries a new rhythm and a new expressive language, filled with freshness and emotion." See Guillermo de Torre, *Literaturas europeas de vanguardia* (Madrid: Rafael Caro Raggio, 1925), p. 388.

15. Lacosta, *op. cit.*, pp. 197–210.

16. In Maeztu's words: "a Don Juan in love is no longer a Don Juan." See Ramiro de Maeztu's interesting essay on this subject, "Don Juan o el Poder," in *Don Quijote, Don Juan y La Celestina: Ensayos en simpatía* (Madrid: Espasa-Calpe, Colección Austral Núm. 31, 1957), pp. 71–106.

17. This process is defined by Henri Bergson in his *Laughter, An Essay on the Meaning of the Comic* (London, 1911), pp. 94–96.

18. Nora, *op. cit.*, p. 252.

19. This amusing fact is contributed by Evaristo Acevedo, in *Teoría e interpretación del humor español* (Madrid: Editora Nacional, 1966), p. 246.

20. An additional source for Jardiel's inspiration and directly concerned with *The Tour of God* is the French novel *Les Mémoires de Dieu-le-Père*, by Pierre Henri Cami (Paris: Editions Baudinrère, 1930). This book, written in the form of a journal of God's memoirs about human deeds and misdeeds, appeared two years before Jardiel published his novel.

Chapter Five

1. Martin Esslin, *The Theatre of the Absurd* (New York: Anchor Books, 1961), p. 247.

2. Remarks conveyed in personal correspondence with Lauro Olmo, June 24, 1972.

3. Remarks conveyed in personal communication with Adolfo Prego, April 11, 1972.

4. See Angel Laborda, "Jardiel Poncela, un autor de hoy," *ABC* (Madrid, March 29, 1972).

5. See Jesús Torre Franco, "¿Qué pudo Enrique Jardiel Poncela?: Una encuesta," in *Estafeta Literaria*, No. 340 (Madrid, March 26, 1966), p. 8.

6. Remarks conveyed in personal correspondence with Antonio Buero Vallejo, April 8, 1972.

7. Remarks conveyed in personal correspondence with Alfonso Sastre, June 8, 1972. Sastre's endorsement of Jardiel's importance was much stronger several years earlier. He devotes an entire chapter to Jardiel in his critical work, *Drama y sociedad* (Madrid: Taurus, 1956), citing him as a *maestro*. Sastre lauds his professional wisdom and his knowledge of theater craft. See *op. cit.*, p. 193.

8. Mihura emphatically repudiates this role. He proudly disclaims any predecessor. See D. R. McKay, *The Avant-garde Theater of Miguel Mihura* (Michigan State University, 1968. Doctoral thesis), pp. 9–32.

9. Remarks conveyed in personal interview with Miguel Mihura, April 26, 1972.

10. See Jesús Torre Franco, p. 9.

11. Remarks conveyed in personal correspondence with José María Pemán, June 12, 1972.

12. Remarks conveyed in personal correspondence with Joaquín Calvo Sotelo, April 12, 1972.

13. The last mentioned playwright—Alonso Millán—has affirmed his indebtedness to Jardiel numerous times and considers himself a true disciple of Jardiel.

14. Remarks conveyed in personal correspondence with Alfredo Marqueríe, April 5, 1972.

15. *Ibid.*

16. Opinion of Joaquín Calvo Sotelo, expressed in aforementioned correspondence, April 12, 1972.

17. Opinion of Alfredo Marqueríe, expressed in aforementioned correspondence, April 5, 1972.

Selected Bibliography

PRIMARY SOURCES

See also Appendix which contains a list of Jardiel Poncela's individual plays and other published or unpublished works, arranged chronologically.

Selected Editions

JARDIEL PONCELA, ENRIQUE. *Obras completas* (Barcelona: Editorial AHR, 1965) 4 vols. Volume One contains eleven of the comedies found in the first five play collections that Jardiel published between 1933 and 1942, with their corresponding prologues plus three one-act playlets. Pages 7–17 consist of an elegiac and eulogistic Introduction by Rámon Gómez de la Serna. Volume Two contains the balance of the major plays and the prologues published between 1942 and 1946. Volume Three consists of miscellaneous short writings, novelettes, maxims, and anecdotes, including *El libro del convaleciente, Exceso de equipaje, Lectura para analfabetos,* and one of his earliest short novels, *El plano astral.* Volume Four brings together the author's four major novels.

————. *Obra inédita* (Barcelona: Editorial AHR, 1967). A collection of miscellaneous short stories, essays, lectures, articles, and reminiscences.

————. *Obras teatrales escogidas* (Madrid: Aguilar, 1964). Contains eighty-seven "Reflexiones teatrales" and the text of nine major plays.

SECONDARY SOURCES

ANTLITZ, HORST KASSEL. "Enrique Jardiel Poncela und das Moderne Spanische Theater," *Maske und Kothurn,* I (1965), 55–77. A good synopsis of Jardiel's life and work, including plot summaries of eight plays and some interesting observations on the meaning of the grotesque and the function of psychology in his theater.

ARAGONÉS, JUAN EMILIO. *Teatro español de posguerra* (Madrid: Publicaciones Españolas, 1971). Pages 9–13 deal expressly with Jardiel's theater. A concise summary on the value of the prologues and the extent of the playwright's adversity.

BONET GELABERT, JUAN. *El discutido indiscutible Jardiel Poncela* (Madrid: Biblioteca Nueva, 1946). This book of 252 pages was written in 1945, in Mallorca, while Jardiel was still alive. Devoid of scholarly organization, its choppy structure and redundant content reveal the author's carelessness with his material. Bonet is thoroughly pro-Jardiel and attacks all those who are not.

BORING, PHYLLIS Z. "The Bases of Humor in the Contemporary Spanish Theatre" (University of Florida, 1966). Unpublished doctoral thesis that refers occasionally to specific plays by Jardiel Poncela to illustrate the peculiar nature of current-day Spanish humor.

CANAY, ALBERTO. *Recuerdo y presencia de Enrique Jardiel Poncela* (Buenos Aires: Edición del autor, 1958). A collection of disconnected biographical fragments, poems, and anecdotes. Minimal scholarly value owing to its many factual inconsistencies, but high in human interest.

FLÓREZ, RAFAEL. *Mío Jardiel: Biografía de un hombre que está debajo de un almendro en flor: Enrique Jardiel Poncela* (Madrid: Biblioteca Nueva, 1966). Reputedly the first biography on Jardiel, but disappointing by its accumulation of wearisome platitudes, silly gossip, and many historical inaccuracies. Jardiel's prologues recast in a flourish of prolix erudition. 367 pages.

––––––. "Jardiel Poncela y su cuaderno de bitácora," *La Estafeta Literaria*, No. 364 (February 25, 1967), 5–6. A cursory consideration of Jardiel's upbringing: his parental guidance and schooling.

––––––. "Jardiel Poncela está debajo de un almendro en flor," *La Estafeta Literaria*, No. 389 (February 10, 1968), 39–40. Unrestrained verbiage in praise of Jardiel. Flórez' intoxication with flashy metaphor devitalizes scholarly value.

––––––. *Jardiel Poncela* (Madrid: EPESA, 1969). Useless for scholarly verification of facts about Jardiel or his writings, this book teems with dogmatic, personal opinions thrown together in a hurry. No critical-analytical concerns. 195 pages.

GARCÍA PAVÓN, FRANCISCO. *Textos y escenarios* (Barcelona: Plaza y Janes, 1971). Pages 91–114 include an analysis of *Cuatro corazones con freno y marcha atrás* as part of an essay entitled "Inventiva en el teatro de Jardiel Poncela."

GÓMEZ DE LA SERNA, RAMÓN. "Enrique Jardiel Poncela: 1901–1952. Breve noticia de su vida y obra," *Clavileño*, No. 20 (Marzo–abril, 1953), 54–57. A clear, factual account of Jardiel's life and works.

————. "Prólogo," in Enrique Jardiel Poncela, *Obras completas*, I (Barcelona: AHR, 1965), 7–17. Sensitive, personal observations about the man Jardiel, his triumphs, decline, and death.

HAMMARSTRAND, ROBERT EDWARD. "The Comic Spirit in the Plays of Enrique Jardiel Poncela," (University of California, Berkeley, 1966). An unpublished doctoral thesis which examines Jardiel's use of plot, dialogue, characters, sets, and stage movement. A good summary about Jardiel and the critics and the playwright's influence on Spanish comedy.

LACOSTA, FRANCISCO. "Enrique Jardiel Poncela: El humorismo en su novela," (University of Missouri, 1966). A serious attempt to define the nature and role of humor as it pertains to Jardiel's four major novels.

————. "El humorismo de Enrique Jardiel Poncela," *Hispania*, XLVII, No. 3 (September, 1963), 501–6. A brief study of humor vis-à-vis Jardiel's novelistic techniques.

MARQUERÍE, ALFREDO. *El teatro de Jardiel Poncela* (Bilbao: Ediciones de Conferencias y Ensayos, 1945). A good monograph of forty-seven pages devoted to the vindication of Jardiel as "the first comic author of our time."

————. *Veinte años de teatro en España* (Madrid: Editora Nacional, 1959). Pages 61–73 present a favorable schematic outline of Jardiel's theater production.

————. "Jardiel y el Jardielismo," *La Estafeta Literaria*, No. 312 (February 27, 1965), 18–19. A general effort to pinpoint the meaning and effect of *Jardielismo* in Spanish theater humor.

MONLEÓN, JOSÉ. *Treinta años de teatro de la derecha* (Barcelona: Tusquets Editor, 1971). Several incisive passages concerning Jardiel's role in the postwar theater of Spain. See especially Chapter Four for a discerning comparison between Mihura and Jardiel.

NORA, EUGENIO G. *La novela española contemporánea (1927–1960)*, II (Madrid: Gredos, 1962), 249–54. Briefly considers Jardiel's first three novels as erotic literature and his *La 'tournée' de Dios* as a frustrated effort to attain a transcendental humor.

PAGE, RICHARD J. "Humor in the Plays of Enrique Jardiel Poncela" (University of Illinois, 1974). Unpublished doctoral thesis devoted to an analysis of the characteristic and original elements of humor in Jardiel's theater.

ROF CARBALLO, J., et al. *El teatro de humor en España* (Madrid: Editora Nacional, 1966). Contains four valuable essays on Jardiel: Nicolás González Ruiz, "El teatro de humor del siglo XX hasta Jardiel Poncela," pp. 31–44; Adolfo Prego, "Jardiel ante la sociedad," pp. 45–61; Alfredo Marquerie, "Novedad en el teatro de Jardiel," pp. 63–81; and Francisco García Pavón, "Inventiva en el teatro de Jardiel Poncela," pp. 83–104. Other studies in this extremely useful compilation provide a rich insight into the theater creeds and practices of several of Jardiel's contemporaries.

RUIZ RAMÓN, FRANCISCO. *Historia del teatro español, 2: Siglo XX* (Madrid: Alianza Editorial, 1971). Pages 298–309 present an excellent overview of Jardiel's "aspiration for the inverisimilar," based on sound documentation.

SASTRE, ALFONSO. *Drama y sociedad* (Madrid: Taurus, 1956). A well-written tribute to Jardiel's technical mastery. Also a genuine lament over the premature loss of his creative potential. See Part Four, Chapter Three, pp. 193–95.

TEATRO: Revista Internacional de la Escena, No. 4 (February, 1953), 27–44. Commemorative issue honoring Jardiel on first anniversary of his death. Articles by Mariluz Jardiel Poncela, Eduardo Haro Tecglen, and Ángel Zúñiga. Also includes interview observations by Jardiel, a partial Bibliography and brief Chronology.

TORRE FRANCO, JESUS. "¿Qué pudo Enrique Jardiel Poncela?: Una encuesta," *La Estafeta Literaria*, No. 340 (March 26, 1966), 8–9. Results of a survey conducted among seven individuals concerning Jardiel's present-day importance.

TORRENTE BALLESTER, GONZALO. *Teatro español contemporáneo* (Madrid: Guadarrama, 1957), 249–57. A brief commentary on Jardiel's dramatic method, focusing on *Eloísa está debajo de un almendro*.

Appendix

I Unpublished Plays

A. Repudiated Writings

The following titles represent comedies which exist only in manuscript form. They were never performed and their author energetically repudiated the entire listing.

1. *Gifts Will Overcome All Reluctances (Dádivas quebrantan peñas)*. Two-act comedy. Written in collaboration with Serafín Adame Martínez, 1916.

2. *Malaisian Gold* (El oro de la Malasia). Three acts, 1917.

3. *Winds of the Earth (Aires de la tierra)*. Two acts, 1917.

4. *The Lovers of Teruel (Los amantes de Teruel)*. Three-act comedy parodying the play by Hartzenbusch. Written in collaboration with Serafín Adame Martínez, 1918.

5. *The Castilian Lion (El león castellano)*. A theatrical verse biography of Gonzalo de Córdoba in three acts, 1918.

6. *Nebuchadnezzar's Reign (El reinado de Nabucodonosor)*. One-act comedy. Written in collaboration wtih Serafín Adame Martínez, 1918.

7. *Salucilla*. One act. Written in collaboration with Serafín Adame Martínez, 1918.

8. *Blanca of Bouvines (Blanca de Bouvines)*. One act, 1918.

9. *The Black Gaucho (El gaucho negro)*. Three-act comedy. Written in collaboration with Serafín Adame Martínez, 1919.

10. *Dr. Hasckruck (El doctor Hasckruck)*. Three acts. Written in collaboration with Serafín Adame Martínez, 1919.

11. *The Collegial Church Ghost (El duende de la Colegiata)*. Three acts. Written in collaboration with Serafín Adame Martínez, 1920.

12. *The Azores Mishaps (Los azares de Azores)*. Two acts. Written in collaboration with Serafín Adame Martínez, 1920.

13. *Irene's Precocity (La precocidad de Irene)*. Two acts. Written in collaboration with Serafín Adame Martínez, 1920.

14. *Holy Rafael (El divino Rafael)*. Two acts. Written in collaboration with Serafín Adame Martínez, 1921.

15. *The First Spada* (*El primer Spada*). Two acts. Written in collaboration with Serafín Adame Martínez, 1921.

16. *The Men* (*Los hombres*). Three-act comedy adaptation of a novel by Alberto Insúa, 1922.

17. *To Have a Pretty Wife* (*Tener la mujer bonita*). Two acts. Written in collaboration with Serafín Adame Martínez, 1922.

18. *Red Precipitate* (*El precipitado rojo*). One act. Written in collaboration with Serafín Adame Martínez, 1922.

19. *That's the Way America Is* (*América es así*). One act. Written in collaboration with Serafín Adame Martínez, 1922.

20. *The Eagle's Flight* (*El vuelo del águila*). A five-act biography in verse about the Duke of Gandía. Written in collaboration with Serafín Adame Martínez, 1923.

21. *In the Quiet of the Night* (*En el silencio de la noche*). A four-act comedy adaptation of Gaston Leroux's novel, *Rouletabille en Rusia*. Written in collaboration with Serafín Adame Martínez, 1923.

22. *The Marine Compass* (*La aguja de marear*). One act, 1923.

23. *Life Insurance* (*El seguro de vida*). One act. Written in collaboration with Serafín Adame Martínez, 1923.

24. *The Neighbor Across the Street* (*El vecino de enfrente*). One act, 1923.

25. *The Ox Apis Mummy* (*La momia del buey Apis*). Two acts, 1923.

26. *Newspaper Clippings* (*Recortes de periódico*). Two acts, 1923.

27. *The Monster's Eyes* (*Los ojos del monstruo*). Four-act comedy. Written in collaboration with Serafín Adame Martínez, 1923.

28. *The Other Man's Trail* (*La huella del otro*). Three acts. Written in collaboration with Serafín Adame Martínez, 1923.

29. *An Englishman Who Has Fun* (*Un inglés que se divierte*). Three acts, 1923.

30. *The Humble Pathway* (*El sendero humilde*). Three acts. Written in collaboration with Serafín Adame Martínez, 1923.

31. *Could You Be Colette?* (*¿Pero es usted Colette?*). Three-act comedy, 1923.

32. *Theatrics* (*Teatralerías*). One act. Written in collaboration with Serafín Adame Martínez, 1923.

33. *Vienna* (*La ciudad de Viena*). Two acts. Written in collaboration with Serafín Adame Martínez, 1923.

34. *The Long Dress* (*El vestido largo*). One act, 1923.

35. *Archimedes' Principle* (*El principio de Arquimedes*). One act. Written in collaboration with Serafín Adame Martínez, 1924.

36. *Coach Number 13* (*El coche número 13*). Five-act dramatic adaptation of the novel by Xavier de Montepin, 1924.

37. *In Case of Fire* (*Para caso de incendio*). One act. Written in collaboration with Serafín Adame Martínez, 1924.

38. *The Mad Palace* (*Locura-Palace*). Three-act comedy written in collaboration with José Simón Valdivieso, 1924.

39. *The Neighborhood Sorceress* (*La pitonisa del barrio*). Two acts. Written in collaboration with Serafín Adame Martínez, 1924.

40. *To Rome by All Means* (*A Roma por todo*). One act. Written in collaboration with Serafín Adame Martínez, 1924.

41. *A Reputable Man* (*Un hombre de bien*). Three-act comedy written in collaboration with José López Rubio, 1924.

42. *The Year 2500* (*El año 2500*). Three acts. Written in collaboration with José López Rubio, 1925.

43. *An Unkind Indian* (*Indio sin gracia*). One act, 1925.

44. *Tiby and Dabo* (*Tiby y Dabo*). One act, 1925.

45. *The Chastity Belt* (*El cinturón de castidad*). Two-act comedy written in collaboration with Carlos Sampelayo, 1925.

46. *Welcome, Magellan* (*Bienvenido, Magallanes*). Three acts. Written in collaboration with Serafín Adame Martínez, 1925.

47. *Landrú of Bellas Vistas* (*El Landrú de Bellas Vistas*). One act, 1925.

48. *The Count of Chateron* (*El conde de Chaterón*). Three-act comedy written in collaboration with Serafín Adame Martínez, 1925.

49. *The Young Girl's Cloak* (*El mantón de la "china"*). One act, 1926.

50. *Madame Delfos, from Four to Nine* (*Madame de Delphos, de 4 a 9*). Three-act comedy. Manuscript lost during a move of residence in 1927.

51. *The 10:45 Express* (*El rápido de las 10,45*). Three-act comedy. Manuscript lost during a move of residence in 1927.

52. *Rick is a Redskin* (*Rick es un piel roja*). Three acts, 1927.

53. *Don't Blame Anyone for My Death* (*No se culpe a nadie de mi muerte*). Three-act comedy, 1928.

B. Performed but Unpublished Plays

The following comedies were performed on the legitimate stage, but were subsequently repudiated by Jardiel Poncela and not released for publication.

1. *Prince Raudhick* (*El príncipe Raudhick*). A four-act whodunit farce, written in collaboration with Serafín Adame Martínez. Bilbao, Teatro Trueba, 1919.

2. *The Saboya Gang* (*La banda de Saboya*). One-act and four-

scene lyrical parody on mystery dramas. Written in collaboration with
Serafín Adame Martínez. Madrid, Teatro Novedades, 1922.

3. *My Cousin Dolly* (*Mi prima Dolly*). Three acts. Written in collaboration with Serafín Adame Martínez. Mexico, Teatro Colón, 1923.

4. *Move on in, It suits Your Interest!* (*¡Achanta, que te conviene!*).
Madrilenean musical sketch. Written in collaboration with Serafín
Adame Martínez. Music by Modesto Romero. Madrid, Teatro Romea,
1925.

5. *The Bonfire* (*La hoguera*). Three-act drama based on a short
story by Andreiev. Written in collaboration with Serafín Adame
Martínez. Madrid, Teatro Infanta Isabel, 1925.

6. *He Winked At You!* (*¡Te ha guiñado un ojo!*). Spanish version
of Hennequin and Weber's comedy, *Et moi j't'dis qu'elle t'fait de
l'oeil*. Written in collaboration with Serafín Adame Martínez. Madrid,
Teatro de la Princesa, 1925.

7. *Subway Night* (*La noche del Metro*). Three-act farce. Written
in collaboration with Ernesto Polo. San Sebastián, Teatro Victoria
Eugenia, 1925.

8. *Wenceslao's Trick* (*El truco de Wenceslao*). Lyrical sketch.
Music by Felipe Orejón. Madrid, Teatro Romea, 1926.

9. *What a Columbus!* (*¡Qué Colón!*). Historical musical sketch
written in collaboration with Serafín Adame Martínez. Music by
Rafael Calleja. Madrid, Teatro Romea, 1926.

10. *Room for Rent* (*Se alquila un cuarto*). Comic-lyrical sketch.
Music by Fabre e Insúa. San Sebastián, Teatro Principal, 1926.

11. *Ferdinand the Saint* (*Fernando el Santo*). Musical comedietta.
Written in collaboration with Serafín Adame Martínez. Music by
José María Muñoz. Barcelona, Teatro Trivoli, 1926.

II *Published Plays*

A. Collections

1. *Three Comedies With One Essay* (*Tres comedias con un
solo ensayo*). Madrid: Biblioteca Nueva, 1933.

2. *Angelina, or A Brigadier's Honor* (*Angelina, o El honor de un
brigadier*). Madrid: Biblioteca Nueva, 1935.

3. *Forty-nine Characters Who Found Their Author* (*Cuarenta y
nueve personajes que encontraron a su autor*). Madrid: Biblioteca
Nueva, 1936.

4. *Two Farces and One Operetta* (*Dos farsas y una opereta*).
Madrid: Biblioteca Nueva, 1939.

5. *One Protested Draft and Two at Sight* (*Una letra protestada
y dos letras a la vista*). Madrid: Biblioteca Nueva, 1942.

6. *Three Projectiles From '42 (Tres proyectiles del 42)*. Madrid: Biblioteca Nueva, 1944.

7. *From Blanca to the Cat by Way of the Boulevard (De "Blanca" al "gato", pasando por el "bulevar")*. Madrid: Biblioteca Nueva, 1946.

8. *Water, Oil and Gasoline and Two Other Explosive Mixtures (Agua, aceite y gasolina y otras dos mezclas explosivas)*. Madrid: Biblioteca Nueva, 1946.

B. Individual Comedies

The following listing, briefly annotated, includes all of Jardiel Poncela's performed, published, and acknowledged plays. Each date represents the play's première.

1. *A Sleepless Spring Night (Una noche de primavera sin sueño)*. Humorous three-act comedy. Jardiel's first important stage success. A husband's scheme to save his marriage nearly backfires. Madrid, Teatro Lara, May 28, 1927.

2. *Señor García's Cadaver (El cadáver del señor García)*. Three-act mediocre farce. The apparent suicide over a case of unrequited love gives rise to a long series of equivocal situations. Madrid, Teatro de la Comedia, February 21, 1930.

3. *Margarita, Armando, and His Father (Margarita, Armando y su padre)*. Four-act parody of Alexandre Dumas' romantic drama, *La Dame aux camélias*. Conventionally structured and unrepresentative of Jardiel's theater, it concerns the degeneration of a romantic relationship into boredom. Madrid, Teatro de la Comedia, April 17, 1931.

4. *You Have the Eyes of a Fatal Woman (Usted tiene los ojos de mujer fatal)*. Three-act comedy adaptation of Jardiel's third novel, *Eleven Thousand Virgins*. The amorous exploits of a modern Don Juan. Madrid, Teatro Cervantes, September 20, 1932.

5. *Angelina, or A Brigadier's Honor (Angelina, o El honor de un brigadier)*. Three acts. Subtitled "A Drama of 1880," this well-balanced caricature in verse is a good parody of nineteenth-century melodrama, particularly the neo-Romantic theater of Echegaray. Madrid, Teatro Infanta Isabel, March 2, 1934.

6. *A Proper Adultery (Un adulterio decente)*. Three acts. An artificial comedy dealing with a doctor's miracle cure for adultery. Madrid, Teatro Infanta Isabel, May 2, 1935.

7. *Satan's Five Warnings (Las cinco advertencias de Satanás)*. Four acts. A finely-constructed comedy concerning five diabolic predictions that affect the life of an aging Don Juan. Madrid, Teatro de la Comedia, December 20, 1935.

8. *Four Hearts in Check and Backward March* (*Cuatro corazones con freno y marcha atrás*). Three acts. An exceptionally well-written farce, originally entitled *Dying is a Mistake* (*Morirse es un error*). A miracle drug stops the aging process, but its benefactors find immortality a bore. Madrid, Teatro Infanta Isabel, May 2, 1936.

9. *Carlo Monte in Montecarlo* (*Carlo Monte en Montecarlo*). A lavish operetta in fourteen tableaux about the adventures of a notorious, inveterate gambler. Music by Jacinto Guerrerro. Madrid, Teatro Infanta Isabel, June 16, 1939.

10. *A Round-Trip Husband* (*Un marido de ida y vuelta*). Three acts. An amusing farce with a striking similarity to Noel Coward's *Blithe Spirit* (1941). A ghost returns to reprove his wife for remarrying. Madrid, Teatro Infanta Isabel, October 21, 1939.

11. *Heloise Lies Under an Almond Tree* (*Eloísa está debajo de un almendro*). One prologue and two acts. A titillating, dazzling comedy about a family's bewildering search for the meanings of suspected crimes. This play marks the high point of *Jardielismo*. Madrid, Teatro de la Comedia, May 24, 1940.

12. *Love Lasts Only 2000 Meters* (*El amor sólo dura 2.000 metros*). Five acts. A superficial melodrama about the misadventures of a Hollywood film writer and a famous actress. Madrid, Teatro de la Comedia, January 22, 1941.

13. *We Thieves Are Honorable People* (*Los ladrones somos gente honrada*). Prologue and two acts. A delightful mystery play built on reversals and extreme complications. Thieves collaborate with police to solve a crime. Madrid, Teatro de la Comedia, April 15, 1941.

14. *Mother, The Father Drama* (*Madre, el drama padre*). Prologue and two acts. A delirious caricature of modern melodramas concerning the marriage of four sets of twins to each other. Madrid, Teatro de la Comedia, December 10, 1941.

15. *It's Dangerous to Look Outside* (*Es peligroso asomarse al exterior*). Prologue and two acts. Satire on many popular writings of psychological love adventures. An insipid play about a woman engaged to three men. Madrid, Teatro de la Comedia, April 15, 1942.

16. *The Inhabitants of the Uninhabited House* (*Los habitantes de la casa deshabitada*). Prologue and two acts. A comic mystery drama concerning the attempt of a counterfeit gang to frighten away intruders in a haunted house. Madrid, Teatro de la Comedia, September 29, 1942.

17. *Blanca on the Outside and Rosa Within* (*Blanca por fuera y Rosa por dentro*). Two acts. A carnivalesque farce developed with a crescendo of madness. It deals with the tempestuous battles between

a man and his irascible wife. A masterpiece of Jardielesque inventiveness. Madrid, Teatro de la Comedia, February 16, 1943.

18. *The Cat's Seven Lives* (*Las siete vidas del gato*). Four prologues and two acts. A well-made melodrama of suspense about the latest victim of a long-term family curse. Madrid, Teatro Infanta Isabel, October 10, 1943.

19. *At Six O'Clock on the Corner of the Boulevard* (*A las seis, en la esquina del bulevar*). One act. An amusing *entremés* in two parts about a wife's discovery that her husband is untrustworthy. Cartagena, Cinema Alcázar, July 16, 1943.

20. *You and I Make Three* (*Tú y yo somos tres*). Two acts. Buffoonery surpasses literary substance in this "psychological" farce about the extravagant antics of a bridegroom and his Siamese twin. Madrid, Teatro Infanta Isabel, March 16, 1945.

21. *The Wandering Lady's Handkerchief* (*El pañuelo de la dama errante*). Two acts. An enigmatic and unsubstantial tragicomedy about a floating ghost and a poor girl who becomes an heiress. Madrid, Teatro de la Comedia, October 5, 1945.

22. *The Love of the Cat and the Dog* (*El amor del gato y del perro*). One act. A good *paso* based on a dialogue between a young girl searching for the meaning of love and a middle-aged man who helps her find it. Madrid, Teatro de la Comedia, December 5, 1945.

23. *Water, Oil and Gasoline* (*Agua, aceite y gasolina*). Four acts. A low comedy of dubious literary value dealing with the amorous involvement of a famous writer with a married woman. Madrid, Teatro de la Zarzuela, February 27, 1946.

24. *The Weaker Sex Has Undergone Gymnastics* (*El sexo débil ha hecho gimnasia*). Two acts. An underrated fine tragicomedy in two parts, in verse and in prose, about the modern-day emancipation of women in contrast to their nineteenth-century bondage. Madrid, Teatro de la Comedia, October 4, 1946.

25. *Blondes Go Better with Potatoes* (*Como mejor está las rubias es con patatas*). Prologue and two acts. A ludicrous, frivolous play about the presumed metamorphosis of a noted scientist into a cannibal. Madrid, Teatro Cómico, December 6, 1947.

26. *Tigers Hidden in the Bedroom* (*Los tigres escondidos en la alcoba*). Two acts. Jardiel's last play, a work of preposterous incongruity. It concerns the assault of a band of international jewel thieves on a luxury hotel. Madrid, Teatro Gran Vía, January 21, 1949.

C. Monologues

1. *Hollywood Intimacies* (*Intimidades de Hollywood*). Performed by Catalina Bárcena in Madrid, Teatro Coliseum, 1935.

2. *The Woman and the Automobile* (*La mujer y el automóvil*). Performed by Catalina Bárcena in Madrid, Teatro Coliseum, 1935.

3. *The Dance* (*El baile*). Performed by Catalina Bárcena in Madrid, Teatro Coliseum, 1935.

4. *Professional Tales and Gossip* (*Cuentos y chismes del oficio*). Performed by Isabel Garcés in Madrid, Teatro Infanta Isabel, 1939.

5. *In the Light of the Large Window* (*A la luz del ventanal*). Performed by María Paz Molinero in Barcelona, Teatro Barcelona, 1946.

6. *Why Would I Want a Monument?* (*¿Para qué quiero un monumento?*). Verse monologue, unperformed, written in 1948.

III *Major Novels*

A. Unpublished Writings, Repudiated by Jardiel Poncela

1. *Monsalud of Brievas* (*Monsalud de Brievas*). Romantic historical novel written at the age of eleven, 1917.

2. *Voice of Alarm* (*La voz de alarma*). 1918.

3. *The Last Will and Testament of Jonas Clay* (*El testamento de Jonás Clay*). 1923

4. *The Bullet Wound* (*El balazo*). 1924.

5. *Valentina's Prayer Book* (*El devocionario de Valentina*). 1925.

B. Published Works

1. *Love Is Written Without the Letter 'H'* (*Amor se escribe sin hache*). A lengthy parody on the exaggerations of popular novels of romance and eroticism. (Madrid: Editorial Biblioteca Nueva, 1929).

2. *Wait for Me In Siberia, My Love* (*Espérame en Siberia, vida mía*). Whimsical parody on romantic adventure travels (Madrid: Biblioteca Nueva, 1930).

3. *Eleven Thousand Virgins* (*Pero . . . ¿hubo alguna vez once mil vírgenes?*). Mocking satire about a sentimental Don Juan (Madrid: Biblioteca Nueva, 1931).

4. *The Tour of God* (*La 'tournée' de Dios*). A bittersweet burlesque on human folly. The Supreme Being visits mankind and is rejected. Jardiel's best novel. (Madrid: Biblioteca Nueva, 1932).

IV *Short Novels*

1. *The Case of Sir Horatio Wilkins* (*El caso de Sir Horacio Wilkins*). Madrid: *La Correspondencia de España*, 1919. Also titled *The Man of Ice* (*El hombre de hielo*) when republished in Madrid: *La Novela Misteriosa*, 1922.

2. *Samotratia's Victory* (*La victoria de Samotracia*). Madrid: *La Correspondencia de España*, 1919.

3. *The Blonde Lady* (*La dama rubia*). Madrid: *La Correspondencia de España*, 1920.

4. *The Dead Voice* (*La voz muerta*). Madrid: *La Novela Misteriosa*, 1922.

5. *The Dreadful Secret of Máximo Marville* (*El espantoso secreto de Máximo Marville*). Madrid: *La Novela Misteriosa*, 1922.

6. *A Strange Adventure* (*Una aventura extraña*). Madrid: *La Novela Misteriosa*, 1922.

7. *Vadi's Smile* (*La sonrisa de Vadi*). Madrid: *La Novela Misteriosa*, 1922.

8. *The Telephone Warning* (*El aviso telefónico*). *La Novela Misteriosa*, 1922.

9. *Silence* (*El silencio*). Madrid: *La Novela Misteriosa*, 1922.

10. *Two White Hands* (*Dos manos blancas*). Madrid: *La Novela Misteriosa*, 1922.

11. *The Footprints* (*Las huellas*). Madrid: *La Novela Misteriosa*, 1922.

12. *The Mystery of the Black Triangle* (*El misterio del triángulo negro*). Madrid: *La Correspondencia de España*, 1922.

13. *Adventures of Torthas and Pan Pin Tao* (*Aventuras de Torthas y Pan Pin Tao*). Madrid: *La Correspondencia de España*, 1922.

14. *The Astral Plane* (*El plano astral*). Madrid: *La Correspondencia de España*, 1922. This novelette was accorded a recommendation by the Madrid Círculo de Bellas Artes.

15. *The Hallucinating Girl* (*La muchacha de las alucinaciones*). Madrid: *La Novela de Amor*, 1924.

16. *Hell* (*El infierno*). Madrid: *La Novela de Amor*, 1924.

17. *The Man Alexandra Loved* (*El hombre a quien amó Alejandra*). Madrid: *La Novela Pasional*, 1924.

18. *Fragrant Simplicity* (*La sencillez fragante*). Madrid: *Nuestra Novela*, 1925.

19. *Defenses of the Mind* (*Las defensas del cerebro*). Madrid: *Nuestra Novela*, 1925.

20. *An Inconsistency* (*Una ligereza*). Madrid: *La Novela de Amor*, 1925.

21. *Lucretia and Mesalina* (*Lucrecia y Mesalina*). Madrid: *La Novela de Amor*, 1925.

22. *The Open Door* (*La puerta franqueada*). Madrid:: *Nuestra Novela*, 1926.

23. *Eight Months of Love* (*Ocho meses de amor*). Madrid: *Nuestra Novela*, 1926.

24. *Jack the Ripper* (*Jack, el destripador*). Madrid: *La Novela Vivida*, 1926.

25. *The Olympic Games of Bellas Vistas* (*La Olimpiada de Bellas Vistas*). Madrid: *La Novela Deportiva*, 1926.

26. *The Infamous Acts of a Viscount* (*Las infamias de un vizconde*). Madrid: Buen Humor, 1926.

27. *The 38 Murders and a Half of the Castle of Hull* (*Los 38 asesinatos y medio del Castillo de Hull*). Madrid: *Los once*, 1935.

28. *The Shipwreck of "The Mistinguette"* (*El naufragio del "Mistinguette"*). San Sebastián: *Los Novelistas*, 1938.

29. *Ten Minutes to Midnight* (*Diez minutos antes de la medianoche*). San Sebastián: *Los Novelistas*, 1939.

In addition to the above titles, many articles and short stories were published by Jardiel between 1919 and 1937 in various journals and periodicals, including: *Aire Libre, Blanco y Negro, Buen Humor, Comedias, Chiquilín, Domingo, Gutiérrez, Heraldo de Madrid, Informaciones, El Liberal, La Libertad, Los Lunes* de *El Imparcial, Mundo Gráfico, La Nueva Humanidad, Nuevo Mundo, Ondas, La Opinión, Las Provincias, El Sol, La Voz.*

V   Miscellaneous Books

1. *A Prodigal Son* (*Un hijo prodigal*). Translation of the novel by Tristan Bernard (Madrid: Editorial Rivadeneyra, 1923).

2. *Procreation and Birth* (*La proceación y el parto*). Translation of book by Dr. Cavfeynon (Madrid: Editorial Caro Raggio, 1923).

3. *Pirulís of Havana* (*Pirulís de la Habana*). A collection of short stories (Madrid: Editorial Popular, 1927).

4. *The Convalescent's Book* (*El libro del convaleciente*). A miscellany of quips, anecdotes, playlets, and humorous stories (Zaragoza: Colección Hispania, 1938).

5. *Readings for the Illiterate* (*Lecturas para analfabetos*). A collection of fifteen short stories (Madrid:: Editorial Biblioteca Nueva, 1938).

6. *Excess Baggage* (*Exceso de equipaje*). A compilation of reminiscences, stories, articles, short plays, lectures, novelettes, and travel yarns (Madrid:: Editorial Biblioteca Nueva, 1943).

VI   Major Lectures

A.   Public Lectures

1. "Consequences of a Highway Trip on Six Wheels" ("Con-

secuencias de un viaje por carretera en sexticiclo"). Zaragoza, Casino Mercantil, 1927.

2. "From Paris to Hollywood in Sixty Minutes" ("De París a Hollywood en sesenta minutos"). Barcelona, Publi-Cinema, 1933.

3. "Woman, An Indispensable Element for Breathing" ("La mujer, como elemento indispensable para la respiración"). Madrid: Residencia de los Estudiantes, 1933.

4. "The Joy of Returning" ("La alegría de volver"). Madrid, Liceo Francés, 1933.

5. "New York and Other North American Small Towns" ("Nueva York y otros pueblecitos de Norteamérica"). San Sebastián, Círculo Artístico, 1933.

6. "How We Laugh in Spain" ("Cómo reímos en España"). Los Angeles, U.C.L.A., 1934.

7. "One Should Laugh at Unfunny Things" ("Hay que reírse de todo lo que no tenga gracia"). San Sebastián, Hospital de Guerra, 1938.

8. "The Theater" ("El Teatro"). Madrid, Sociedad de Antiguos Alumnos del Colegio de San Antón, 1941.

9. "A Greeting to Barcelona" ("Saludo a Barcelona"). Lecture in verse. Barcelona, Teatro Borrás, 1943.

10. "Going and Coming" ("Irse y volver"). Buenos Aires, Teatro Cómico, and Montevideo, Teatro Artigas, 1944.

11. "The Life of Art and the Art of Life" ("La vida del arte y el arte de la vida"). Universidad de Valladolid, 1946.

B. Radio Lectures

1. "Fortnightly Commentaries for Informal Listeners" ("Comentarios quincenales para oyentes informales"). Bimonthly radio broadcasts over Madrid's Union Radio, 1926–1928.

2. "The Worst Things in the World Are Men and Women" ("Lo peor que hay en el mundo son los hombres y las mujeres"). Madrid, Union Radio, 1929.

3. "The Heroic Summer Vacations in the Sierra" ("Los veraneos heroicos en la Sierra"). Madrid, Union Radio, 1929.

4. Nine lectures over Buenos Aires' Radio Rivadavia, 1937: "Do You Give your permission?" ("¿Dan ustedes su permiso?"); "Marriage" ("El matrimonio"); "Woman" ("La mujer"); "Man" ("El hombre"); "Travels" ("Viajes"); "More Travels" ("Más viajes"); "And Still More Travels" (Y todavía más viajes"); "With Your Permission" ("Con permiso de ustedes").

VII Movie Scripts

1. *That's My Man* (*Es mi hombre*). An adaptation of Carlos Arniches' "grotesque tragedy" of the same name. Movie directed by Fernández Cuenca. Madrid, 1927.

2. *A Prisoner Has Escaped* (*Se ha fugado un preso*). Directed by Benito Perojo. Madrid, 1931.

3. *Wild Girl* (*Joven silvestre*). Spanish adaptation and dialogue. Fox Film Corporation, Hollywood, 1932.

4. *Six Hours to Live* (*Seis horas para vivir*). Spanish adaptation and dialogue. Fox Film Corporation, Hollywood, 1932.

5. *Gypsy King* (*El rey de los gitanos*). Spanish adaptation and dialogue. Fox Film Corporation, Hollywood, 1932.

6. *The Forbidden Melody* (*La melodía prohibida*). Spanish adaptation and dialogue. Fox Film Corporation, Hollywood, 1932.

7. *Rancid Celluloid* (*Celuloide rancio*). Jardiel's first series of spoken commentary added to silent films. The series includes "The Great Train Robbery" ("Los expresos y el ex preso"); "The Heart of Waleska" ("Ruskaia gunai zominovitz"); "Twin Dukes and a Duchess" ("El calvario de un hermano gemelo"); "Emma's Dilemma" ("Emma, la pobre rica"); "For the Man She Loved" ("El amor de una secretaria"); "The Chorus Girl" ("Cuando los bomberos aman"). Produced by Fox Movietone Corporation, Billancourt (Paris), 1933.

8. *Pursued* (*Perseguido*). Spanish adaptation and dialogue. Fox Film Corporation, Hollywood, 1934.

9. *Hold Fast to Your Wife* (*Asegure a su mujer*). Spanish adaptation and dialogue for a French film translated by Julio Escobar, Fox Film Corporation, Hollywood, 1934.

10. *Angelina, or A Brigadier's Honor* (*Angelina, o El honor de un brigadier*). Spanish film adaptation of Jardiel's play. Directed by Jardiel Poncela. Fox Film Corporation, Hollywood, 1934.

11. *You Have the Eyes of a Fatal Woman* (*Usted tiene los ojos de mujer fatal*). Spanish film adaptation of Jardiel's play. Directed by Horacio Socías. Barcelona, 1937.

12. *Margarita, Armando and His Father* (*Margarita, Armando y su padre*). Spanish film version of Jardiel's play. Directed by Francisco Mugica. "Lumiton," Buenos Aires, 1937.

13. *Comic Celluloids* (*Celuloides cómicos*). Jardiel's second series of spoken commentary added to silent films. The series includes: "Definitions" ("Definiciones"); "Signs" ("Letreros"); "One Advertisement and Five Letters" ("Un anuncio y cinco cartas"); "Rodriros the Fakir" ("El faquir Rodriros"). Produced by Cea Studios, San Sebastián, 1938.

14. *Maurice, or A Victim of Vice* (*Mauricio, o Una víctima del vicio*). A new version of the 1912 film, *The Green Curtain* (*La cortina verde*). Directed by Jardiel Poncela. Ballesteros Productions, Madrid, 1940.

15. *Love Is a Microbe* (*El amor es un microbio*). Film adaptation of Jardiel's comedy, *A Proper Adultery* (*Un adulterio decente*). Buenos Aires, "Lumiton" Corporation, 1944.

The following titles of plays and one novel have been filmed without the playwright's direct intervention. Spain: *Los ladrones somos gente honrada* (Ignacio F. Iquino, Director), 1941; *Eloísa está debajo de un almendro* (Rafael Gil, Director), 1943; *Los habitantes de la casa deshabitada* (Gonzalo Delgras, Director), 1946; *Tú y yo somos tres* (Rafael Gil, Director), 1961. Mexico: *Usted tiene ojos de mujer fatal* (José María Elorrieta, Director), 1962; *Las cinco advertencias de Satanás*, n.d.; *¡Espérame en Siberia, vida mía*, n.d.; *Un marido de ida y vuelta* (Luis Lucia, Director), 1957.

Index

(The works of Jardiel Poncela mentioned in the text of this study
are listed under his name)